D1539211

People of God in the Night

The People of God in the Night

by

Eloi Leclerc

Translated by

Paul Lachance and Paul Schwartz

FRANCISCAN HERALD PRESS
1434 WEST 51st STREET ● CHICAGO, 60609

Library of Congress Cataloging in Publication Data

Leclerc, Éloi.
   People of God in the night.

   (Tau series)
   Translation of Le peuple de Dieu dans la nuit.
   1. Christianity—20th century.   I.   Title.
BR121.2.L3513   270.8'2'7   79-1107
ISBN 0-8199-0768-5

NIHIL OBSTAT:
Fr. Theophile Desbonnets
September 13, 1976
IMPRIMI POTEST:
Fr. Frederic Deblock
Minister Provincial
September 16, 1976
IMPRIMATUR:
E. Berrar
Vicar Episcopal
September 30, 1976

Editorial Preface

The "Tau" Series

The Tau was the talisman of St. Francis of Assisi. It takes its shape from Greek letter Tau (T), which is a cross. This method of forming the cross is very ancient, and goes back even to the days of the Old Testament. "Go through the midst of Jerusalem," spoke the Lord God to the destroying angel, "mark Tau upon the foreheads of the men that sigh and mourn for all the abominations that are committed in the midst thereof" (Ezech. 9, 4). Historians generally admit that Francis was present at the Fourth Lateran Council, opened November 11, 1215 at St. John Lateran at which Pope Innocent III gave the opening address. After depicting the profanation of the Holy Places by the Saracens, the Pontiff deplored the scandals dishonoring Christ's flock, threatening it with God's punishments if it did not reform. He recalled Ezekiel's famous vision in which the Lord God, his patience exhausted, cries out in a loud voice: and after quoting the passage

v

above, the Pope continued: "The TAU has exactly the same form as the Cross on which our Lord was crucified on Calvary. And only those will be marked with this sign and will obtain mercy, who have mortified their flesh and conformed their life to that of the Crucified Savior."

How could Francis, who saw God's hand in everything, be other than impressed by this proclamation which expressed so well his ideal of life and his dream of an apostolate. The fact is that the TAU, which the Pope made the emblem of the reform, became from then on Francis' own blazon, talisman and signature.

The TAU SERIES of books is to be published in this spirit. It will endeavor to indicate the extent and the direction of the great Franciscan movement in every field of life and culture. At the same time the series will be geared to interpret the man and the movement in the terms of modern life. For the publisher feels that the greatest danger to St. Francis' fame today is that he should lose reality and become little more than a popular figure in a saintly fairy land.

Contents

Preface

> This strange secret into which God has withdrawn
> himself....
>
> Pascal, Letter to Charlotte de Roannez

I want to dedicate these pages to the men and women who, faced with the current evolution of the world, deeply question themselves and are anxious about the future of faith.

Faith is presently undergoing a very serious crisis. Men and women who have committed their lives to the certainties of faith feel that in their environment and in religious circles themselves, these basic and vital certainties have begun to waver. It is as if each person were left alone to define his or her faith. Thus one should not be surprised that many believers are secretly at a complete loss. They are bewildered by all this drifting which no one seems able to see an end to. It is easier to defend oneself against open persecution than against the hidden and interior forces of disintegration.

1

Faced with this difficult situation, a number of attitudes are possible. The first is to try to hold onto a superficial optimism. "Everything will turn out all right. Countercurrents, shadows, and false steps exist, to be sure; these are unavoidable. But wait a while and you will see; everything will return to order." When one hears these reassuring remarks one cannot help but think of the reflection made by a finance minister who declared on the eve of a de-valutation: "Yes, indeed everything does set itself aright"—adding on the sly, "Occasionally very badly." Some time ago on a television program, a bishop was questioned on current problems of the Church and of faith. To his always courteous questioners whose barbs were carefully blunted, the bishop responded with an obvious sincerity, but also with much—perhaps too much—skill and prudence. The problems of the age were scaled down and then dismissed as if by sleight of hand; once again Peter's bark glided over tranquil waters and "the waves were as transparent as on the fairest of days." But was it really a moment of truth?

Let us have no illusions. The crisis runs too deeply for things to come together so easily. It will no doubt become more and more difficult for a believer simply to be a believer. The believer will find himself more and more isolated in his faith, without exterior support and without signs. It is not necessary to be a prophet to see that this moment is coming and has already come for many. Let us have the courage to say so: night is falling and it is only beginning to do so.

Faced with this crisis of faith a second attitude is

possible; that of despair and panic. "The boat is sinking. Everyone for himself!" This is not shouted from the rooftops; but it is possible that this kind of thinking is going on, without it being acknowledged openly. And covertly everyone plans his or her escape route. We must reject this attitude as unworthy and contrary to a deep faith.

There remains a third and final attitude, the only one worthy of retention. It consists in not submitting to this night but in trying to understand it and pass through it in the light of the word of God. It has to do with accepting it not as a catastrophe but as a mystery full of calling and of meaning which is part of the plan of God. For this "we have the word of the prophets"; and what is required of us is to take this word "as a lamp for lighting a way through the dark until the dawn comes and the morning star rises in our minds." (2 Pet. 1, 19)

What we are called to live today has in fact already been lived in a prophetic way by the people of God at a given moment of its history, precisely during the long exile which followed the national disaster of 587 B.C. This exile, which lasted some fifty years, was a true night crossing for the people of God; it meant the end of an age. The people then experienced the nightfall of their institutions. Everything that formed their framework and protection fell into the shadows. Everything that could give it confidence in its own destiny was destroyed. Jerusalem and its temple were leveled. The kingdom was surpressed, the land occupied and annexed, the elite deported. Stripped of all the special signs that made it the chosen people and dispersed among the pagan nations, Israel was brought back to its primal nakedness. It was driven to face the basic poverty of the person. "Days of darkness and of tumult": this is how the prophet Ezeckiel characterized this time of deportation. Israel no longer knew beforehand who the eternal one was or what he wanted. It had to grope through the night. It is not from the flashing mountaintop of Sinai that the saving word comes, but from the depths of a broken heart.

This experience was lived at such a depth that it transcends the particular historical circumstances within which it unfolded. By touching the deepest part of the person, it attains universality. Certain situations were lived and certain words were said which make this moment of biblical history a prophecy of the deep becoming of the person; for each individual as well as for the entire people of God. Because of this, this experience now concerns us directly. Within it is enclosed the only light which can enlighten our current journey through the night by making us see what we ourselves are called to become.

What becomes of a person when he or she has lost everything, even that which he or she held most sacred? How does one then live one's relationship to the world, to others, and to oneself? To which renewal is one called? And by what way? How can the darkest night become a moment of hope? Through what metamorphosis? All these questions we have asked ourselves while meditating on this great moment of torment for the people of God.

The more a human experience is radical the more it can reveal to us what is fundamental and

eternal. And the biblical experience of exile is one of
the most radical experiences that humanity has ever
undergone. No one can go through such distress
without falling into a bottomless despair unless one
encounters at the bottom of the abyss an indestruc-
tible hope. Today, the people of God need to encounter such a hope.

Chapter 1

The End of a World

... A fugitive arrived from Jerusalem and said to me,
'the city has been taken.' (Ezek. 33, 21)

The day is almost over in Tel-Abib in the canton of
Nippur. This evening, like every other, the deportees from Judah gather around a campfire. They
have worked all day at the canals in the immense
plain watered by the Euphrates. They meet again
now, by themselves, far from their overseers; far
from these men "of barbarous, senseless tongue." (Is.
33, 19) It is a time for relaxation and intimacy. Seat-
ed in a circle, they look at the flame which soars up
in their midst. They say nothing. They share a common experience: weariness, shame, hate, hope. But
especially hope. Life has been tragically simplified
for them: They await.

Deported about ten years ago at the first capture
of Jerusalem by Nebuchadnezzar, they have just
heard about the revolt of King Zedekiah. The news
has rekindled their hopes. The people of Judah has

7

taken up arms again to fight for its freedom. Far away, in the distant homeland, Jerusalem is once more offering up resistance. And Egypt, the almighty Egypt, struggles by its side against the invading Chaldeans. How could one not be hopeful? The hour of victory and of liberation is at hand; it will come more surely than the dawn. More brilliant and all-devouring than the flame. Babylon, Larsa, Nippur—all these great pagan cities will then go up in flames like dry reeds thrown into the fire. Palaces and towers will vanish in smoke. The empire from the Euphrates to the western sea will be in flames.

They await. And already in their dreams they contemplate the dawn heralded by the fire. On that day they will return to their native land; triumphantly they will go up along the course of the great river which they have come down in shame. Like their fathers coming out of Egypt, they will leave loaded with spoils, amid laughter and mouths filled with song. They will see their hillsides again; they will rediscover their towns. Before them the green valley of Akor will open up like a gate of hope. Jerusalem appears on the heights over its ramparts, full of glory: the victorious Jerusalem, free at last! And all its houses shout "Alleluia!" That day is aglow for them already in the flame. And all eyes shine with hope.

And yet on certain evenings the weight of exile seems heavier. News is rare. What is really going on back in the homeland? This evening nostalgia gnaws away in their hearts. A song rises. Sad and solemn, the lament of the exiles begins to drift in the night:

Beside the streams of Babylon
we sat and wept
at the memory of Zion,
leaving our harps
hanging on the poplars there.

For we had been asked
to sing to our captors,
to entertain those who had carried us off:
"Sing," they said,
"some hymns of Zion."

How could we sing
one of Yahweh's hymns
in a pagan country?
Jerusalem, if I forget you,
may my right hand wither! ... (Ps. 137, 1–5)

"Jerusalem"—this name rings loud and clear in the night at Tel-Abib. It crystallizes all their hopes. The resistance of a people is concentrated in it. Jerusalem is the pride of Judah. Power resides there. The house of David is established there. Above all, the temple in which the glory of Yahweh dwells rises there. And all the tribes go up toward the city.

Today, in a country completely overrun, Jerusalem remains sacred and untouched, prepared for a heroic struggle for its freedom. "May peace come inside your city walls! Prosperity to your palaces!" (Ps. 132, 7). No, the deportees have not forgotten it.

In fact, they have not forgotten anything. And above all, they have not forgotten what they have suffered: the long march towards captivity, the endless lines of human beings tied to one another, the shouts and the harassments of the Chaldean soldiers, the endless tracks in the desert. Some of them were sold as slaves in the places they were passing through; others, completely exhausted, were abandoned on the road as fodder for wild beasts. No, they will never forget this. Then their song bursts out with a savage accent. It is no longer simply a lament, but a cry of wrath and vengeance.

> Destructive daughter of Babel.
> a blessing on the man who treats you
> as you have treated us,
> a blessing on him who takes and dashes
> your babies against the rock!... (Ps. 137, 8-9)

The voices no longer make themselves heard. And the silent wait has recommenced. Short flames still dance on the embers. Light white smoke rises straight up. And up above the heavens now shine with all the stars. A milky white heaven which makes one dream of the promised land: its springtime herbs, its golden, gentle hillsides, its white streams leaping like sheep. But abruptly the reverie is broken and their attention brought back to earth. Steps are heard on the road. Human steps. From a distance at first, but coming very close. There is no doubt: there is someone coming. He is walking toward this fire in the night. Heads turn and try to peer through the darkness. A silhouette finally stands out. A man approaches; he is carrying a backpack; his clothing is that of the inhabitants of Judah. All the deportees freeze on the spot. One could hear a grasshopper jump. The man halts a few steps away from the circle of the exiles: "Ah, my brothers!" he exclaims, "I have finally arrived. I come from Jerusalem." At these words all stand. The eldest slowly moves himself toward the newcomer

and greets him in these terms: "Peace on you,
brother, and on Judah. What news do you bring?"

"Brother," the man answers, "there is no peace left:
neither for me nor for Judah."

Emotion combined with weariness prevents the
messenger from saying more. He trembles and lets
his backpack fall on the ground. He would like to
speak but the words stay stuck in his throat. The
exiles press around him; they want to hear. But
there is nothing to hear. Nothing but the panting
breath of hundreds of people standing side by side.
Finally, sobbing, he says these simple words: "The
city is taken."

Stupified, everyone gasps.

"They have burnt it and razed it to the ground,"
continues the man.

"It's not possible!" some voices protest.

"Brothers, I speak to you as an eyewitness. I am
one of the fugitives."

It takes time for a great ship to sink. It takes even
more time for human hearts to be dashed away with
their cargo of hopes.

"And the temple?" one of them asks.

"There is no longer any temple. They set it on fire
after they looted it. They have left nothing standing.
Everything was destroyed. There is nothing left."

Nothing! It is toward this abyss suddenly opened
beneath them that the deportees from Judah inexor-
ably drift. But their reeling hearts still refuse to
believe the irreparable.

"Tell us what happened, brother," asks the eldest
of the community.

The messenger stands stiff as a board. He looks at

no one. Without any gestures, in the same tone of voice, he begins his narrative. "Jerusalem withstood the siege for eighteen months. For a long time we had been waiting to be rescued by the Egyptians. From the top of our towers we were always on the watch. But there was nothing coming, always nothing. They enemy blocked the roads and encircled the city. The population no longer had anything to eat: The reserves of wheat were exhausted. Nor was there any water; the aqueducts were cut off. The plague had hit us and took its toll every day. Already the besiegers and their war machines had advanced up to the ramparts. Battering rams reverberated against the gates of the city. The starved and delirious crowd of refugees pressed together fearfully in the streets. Nevertheless we still hoped for the sudden arrival of the Egyptian army.

"And suddenly we heard that a breach had been made in our walls. King Zedekiah immediately decided to try to escape along with his officers and the rest of his men in the hope of reaching Egypt. He succeeded in slipping out during the night by way of the gate between the two walls close to the garden of the king. All to no avail! The Chaldean troops pursued the king and caught up with him in the plains of Jericho. Abandoned by his men, the king was made prisoner. He was led to Riblah and the general quarters of Nebuchadnezzar. There he was condemned to the punishment due treacherous vassals: his sons were slaughtered before his eyes. Then, with this horrible sight still before him, his eyes were put out and he was taken to Babylon in chains. (cf. 2 Kings 25, 1-7; Jer. 52, 4-11)

"In the meantime, the Chaldeans rushed into Jerusalem and totally ransacked it. For days and days the soldiers killed, looted, and burned. (cf. 2 Kings 25, 8-10; Jer. 52, 12-15) Jerusalem is now in ruins and ashes; the horn of victory sounds over her."

The messenger became silent. The exiles look at one another, stupified. Their emotion is such that they can scarcely say a word. They are like children who have abruptly lost their mother. Their tearful gaze wanders from earth to heaven. All the stars have gone out at once. In their place, infinite emptiness:

> I looked to the earth, to see a formless waste;
> to the heavens, and their light had gone. (Jer. 4, 23)

whose capital was Jerusalem. This division had dangerously weakened the nation in face of Assyrian power which kept growing and extending itself in the Middle East. After the loss of national unity, first Israel and then Judah came under feudal domination. Both had to acknowledge the suzerainity of Assur, then that of Babylon, and had to pay them tribute. In vain did the kingdom of the North try to throw off the yoke: It was purely and simply invaded and annexed. In its turn the kingdom of the South, under the reign of Jehoiakim, revolted a first time. Jerusalem was taken and its king deported with part of the population.

But during this long series of misfortunes the essential had always been preserved: Jerusalem had remained standing throughout the torment; the temple where the glory of Yahweh dwelled had been spared and the kingdom safeguarded. Even on the day following the crushing of Jehoiakim's revolt, a king had been left on the throne of Judah as a vassal. Hopes could be reborn. Too easily and too quickly. This is how Zedekiah, the new king of Judah, conspiring with other vassal nations and aligning himself with Egypt, thought that he could shake off the yoke of Babylon. It was sheer folly.

For decades, the political blindness of the kings of Judah was equaled only by their infidelity to Yahweh and his covenant. The prophets unceasingly raised their voices to lead those responsible for the nation back to the straight path and to a greater foresightedness. They saw disaster and ruin coming. In high places they simply shrugged their shoulders; they taunted these prophets of doom. They were called defeatist and even suspected of treason. What was there to fear at the side of the Egyptian power? Jerusalem, planted on its rock and surrounded by ramparts. was, as they thought, sheltered from all assault. The tactic was a simple and sure one: Let the assailants come, then hold them off until the arrival of the Egyptian army which would smash the troops of Nebuchadnezzar into pieces. And with this, Judah was thrown into the revolt against the Chaldean colossus.

Yet now the unthinkable had occurred. The destruction of Jerusalem and its temple brings Judah all the way down, and with it all of Yahweh's people, handing them over bound hand and foot into the power of their enemies. It is a national catastrophe without precedent. Judah has ceased to exist as a state. The kingdom is destroyed; the land occupied; the elites deported.

New convoys of prisoners take the route of exile toward the East. Leading citizens, public officials, qualified craftsmen, all those capable of exercising influence in the country are led into captivity. After weeks of walking, some will end up in the region of Babylon, others in that of Nippur in southern Mesopotamia.

At Tel-Abib, the days go by in deep sadness. Stupefaction has given way to anxiety. The exiles wonder about their future. What is there left to hope for? They see themselves condemned to live and to die in this foreign land far from their own country, forgotten by heaven and earth. "Our hope has gone. We are as good as dead." (Ezek. 37, 11) This is what they think and mull over day in and day out.

They remember the words of the prophet Jeremiah:

> Do not weep for the man who is dead ...
> Weep bitterly for the man who has gone away,
> since he will never come back,
> never see his native land again (Jer. 22, 10).

Chapter 3
The Prophetic Call

Since the tragic news nothing has changed outwardly in the life of the deportees at Tel-Abib. Their number has simply increased with new arrivals. Old and new people fraternally share the same misfortune. Their situation is one of semifreedom. They are employed in the irrigation works. This immense plain of southern Mesopotamia where the Euphrates flows was once hardly more than a sandy moor. The kings of Babylon have undertaken to fertilize it. Countless canals have been dug. The country is now furrowed with waterways. The fields and horticultural developments prosper. The care of these small artificial rivers requires many qualified workers. The deportees thus pass their days opening and closing the locks, dredging the rivers, draining the bottoms, consolidating the dikes, and digging new waterways. All this under the direction and the control of Chaldean overseers.

Farm work and irrigation are not the only activi-

ties of the deportees. The gloriously reigning
Nebuchadnezzar is a powerful builder. The immense
palace of Babylon, in great part his doing, requires
many workers. The exiles provide them for him. And
the lot of these workers is even harder than that of
their brothers employed in the fields.

The day ended, the exiles return to the barracks in
the villages where fortune has placed them. A freer
life begins for them there: a life among brothers, far
from the pestering of their overseers and the
humiliating gaze of the conqueror. A life where they
try to recover the faces of free persons. They read the
rare letters they might still be getting from other
communities of deportees scattered throughout the
empire, especially the one in Babylon. There, too,
the brothers have learned about the destruction of
Jerusalem and they are raising the same anguishing
questions about their future. They listen to this
news. And they become silent as if at a wake. More
than one of them dreams of the native land, the vil-
lage, the house, the children . . . All this seems so far
away! Far away and unreal. There are no longer any
peaceful villages in Israel, no children's laughter,
no songs on the hillsides. Only the war chariots of
the conquerors rolling across the country. And the
barren hills weeping for their vanished sons and
daughters. There is nothing left in the country ex-
cept a long lament.

Fear has settled inside the hearts of the exiles, the
great fear of those who no longer feel sure of anything. They had been assured of so many things!
They had been convinced that the kingdom of Judah
could confront the Chaldean empire without fear,

that Egypt would support it with its invincible strength, that Jerusalem was impregnable. They had believed all this. And on this certainty they had had starry-eyed dreams. The stars themselves were now fallen. And the land itself slid out from under their feet, the land in which they had rooted their life. Would they be able to see this land again someday? They have the impression that they have been thrown into a void. Uprooted. Nothing shelters them. And when night falls, anguish overcomes and submerges them like an enormous wave in the dark.

Facing more than they can bear, they cry out for justice: "Is this just?" And they go back over the same words: "The fathers have eaten unripe grapes; and the children's teeth are set on edge. Our fathers have sinned and they are dead; and we have to carry the weight of their iniquities. Is this just?" The deportees from Judah seek to escape from the anguish of their hearts. They accuse their fathers and blaspheme Yahweh. But one day a voice rises from among them: "Why do you keep repeating this proverb in the land of Israel: 'The fathers have eaten unripe grapes; and the children's teeth are set on edge'? As I live—it is the Lord Yahweh who speaks—there will no longer be any reason to repeat this proverb in Israel ... A son will not have to carry the sins of his father nor the father the sins of his son ... But if the wicked man renounces all the sins he has committed, respects my laws and is law-abiding and honest, he will certainly live; he will not die. What! Am I likely to take pleasure in the death of a wicked man—it is the Lord Yahweh who speaks—and not prefer to see him renounce his wickedness and live? ... And yet the House of Israel objects, 'What the Lord does is unjust ... House of Israel ... make yourselves a new heart and a new spirit! Why are you so anxious to die, House of Israel? I take no pleasure in the death of anyone—it is the Lord Yahweh who speaks. Repent and live!" (Ezek. 18; 33, 10–20).

This voice which has just made itself heard is that of the prophet Ezekiel, himself one of the first deportees. For a long time the prophet had remained silent. But the Lord Yahweh had told him that on the day a fugitive would come to announce the tragic news of the fall of Jerusalem he would speak again and he would then become a song for his exiled compatriots.

"Why are you anxious to die?" Ezekiel pronounced these words in the name of Yahweh. And now that they have gone out of his mouth and are in some way before him, he realizes how strange they are. He is no doubt the first one to be astonished. Up until this day he had only opened his mouth to foretell misfortune after misfortune. War, invasion, the ruin of Jerusalem, the deportation: all this he had been charged with announcing to the people. When the Lord called him to deliver his message, he made him eat a scroll on which was written on back and front: "lamentations, wailings, moanings" (Ezek. 2, 10).

Ezekiel had devoured this scroll and it had tasted sweeter than honey. But now, only the galling taste of misfortune was on his tongue. While his compatriots lived in a carefree optimism, he was in a state of despair. War, ruin, and death—he saw them roaming at the gates sniffing out their prey; and he lived in this ominous company. Under a seemingly cloudless sky he was brandishing his warnings of the coming terror like a big black flag. And now that everything is in ruin and he no longer has any hope, he cries out to his brothers in exile: "Why are you so anxious to die?"

He, the prophet of doom to whom God had said, "I am going to make your resolution as hard as a diamond and diamond is harder than flint" (Ezek. 3, 9), now stretches out his hand to rescue his fellow campanions in misfortune. He invites them to come up out of the pit. He urges them to believe still in life; it is to live here and now that they have been called, not to die. Yahweh takes no pleasure in the death of anyone (Ezek. 18, 32; 33, 10–20); he wants everyone to live, just and sinner alike.

And Ezekiel shows them the way of their resurrection: "Make yourselves a new heart and a new spirit . . ." (Ezek. 18, 31). These words are simple, disconcertingly so. It has been pointed out that "the most essential things that have been told to humanity have always been simple things.... And what they bring to birth is always unpredictable" (André Malroux, *Les chênes que l'on abat*).

Henceforth, the pillar of religious life, that on which the latter must wholly lean, is no longer the temple, or Jerusalem, or sacrifices, or the holocausts: it is no longer even the nation or the social groups; it is the *heart*, that is to say what is the most intimate, the deepest, and the most personal in men and women. What is most durable also. When everything is lost, the heart remains. It is from there and from there alone that life can begin again.

But it will only begin again out of a heart completely remade. "Make yourself a new heart": these words are a call to a renewal in depth. They send the person back to the mysterious power of renewal that dwells in his own heart. In this power an opportunity for salvation and grace for resurrection is always available. It's up to each person to grasp this opportunity and this grace. It is up to each man and woman to personally decide either for renewal or for decline, for life or for death. It is not the nation which can decide. No one can decide for anyone else. And nothing is decided ahead of time or once and for all. Each person at every moment can and must choose. And no matter what his or her past is, he or she can at every moment either be reborn or die. It depends on him or her alone. "But if the wicked man renounces all the sins he has committed ... he will certainly live; he will not die. All the sins he committed will be forgotten from then on ..." (Ezek. 18, 21–22). "But if the upright man renounces his integrity, commits sin, copies the wicked man and practices every kind of filth, is he to live? All the integrity he has practiced shall be forgotten from then on ..." (Ezek. 18, 24) The relationship of the person with God no longer depends on clan or nation. Henceforth, it rests uniquely on what is the most intimate in each one: the deep orientation of the heart. Each one can at every moment begin a new future.

The deportees from Judah are invited, therefore, to get in touch with their deepest being. But are they capable of hearing such a language? They are so far away from their own hearts! They sent them off so

long ago—ever since they started dreaming of glory.
And now that these dreams have dissipated, they
find themselves estranged, far from the destroyed
towns, from their devastated land—far from their
hearts especially. The deportees look at Ezekiel.
They do not understand. None of them yet feels responsible for his own heart. They look to each other
to know how to act. They have always acted as a
group. And the group was the national collectivity
with its traditions, its institutions, its structures, its
kin, chief, leaders, and its king. These were its conscience, its good and bad conscience. It dispensed
them from inhabiting their own hearts.

But today there is no longer any nation for them.
All the institutions that had framed and sustained
the people have collapsed, even the most sacred.
There are no longer any kings, leaders, or priests.
Can one still speak of them as a people? It has been
scattered to the four corners of the immense Chaldean empire. They are only men and women left to
the forces of their own hearts. Today it is up to each
one of them to hear and to respond. The son no
longer responds for the father nor the father for the
son. It is up to each one to choose: life or death.

To decide alone. How difficult that is! They have
not learned to use their hearts, to depend on them.
They do not know how to listen, think, or live with
their own heart. They are always listening for outside support. They await. Their religion is still a simple one learnt from others, their god is a god of the
group. They do not know Yahweh with their heart.
They do not understand. They feel alone. They are
afraid.

Afraid of the emptiness. For these men and women, the exile is a desert. Like their fathers coming out of Egypt, they are now thrown into the desert. But today the desert consists in the great solitude of the heart.

All the bonds are broken, those of earth as well as those of heaven. Like a weather vane in the wild winds of anguish, such is the heart of the exiles. From the depths of the night, one of the wretched cried out, "Our hope is dead. We have had it." And the 'desert-owl' responded, "Why are you so anxious to die? The night is full of secrets. Open your heart to the unknown."

The unknown is the future which cries out to be born. It is the spirit that hovers over the waters and beats the waves with his giant wings. He always seems to strike from outside; but he is a calling from within. He bears the face of the other, the stranger, even the enemy; and yet he is intimacy itself, the unexplored depth. He is the creative call within the creature, the irresistible yearning of our being toward something greater.

The hour when men and women no longer know who they are, when they wander like shadows across their own ruins, this hour of great solitude and emptiness is also that of great beginnings. It is the hour when the unknown one comes to visit us, when the future draws us to him. It is the hour when the spirit gives us a sign, for he wants to become in us "a new heart," "a new spirit."

Chapter 4

For Your Sake I Remember

Many events took place in the world during this time, but not at Tel-Abib.

For Israel the course of history has come to an abrupt stop; it has been annihilated. It has been replaced by the void, the nonhistory, the time when nothing happens. The prophet Hosea had foretold these times: "For the sons of Israel will be kept for many days without a king, without a leader, without sacrifice or sacred stone, without ephod or teraphim..." (Hos. 3, 4) These times have arrived. All possibility for political and religious action has been removed from Israel as a nation. And not only can Israel no longer be an agent in history, but history no longer acts in its behalf; the nation is of no concern to it. Nothing happens for it anymore. It is a dead time.

But this nonhistory renders possible a new history. Stripped as a nation of all activity proper to it, of every sign distinctive to it, and at the mercy of pagan nations, the men and women of Israel are invited to return to their hearts. This is the great task which they are all convened to undertake: "I will lead her out into the wilderness and speak to her heart," Yahweh had proclaimed. (Hos. 2, 16)

Time would be needed before the exiles could understand the true meaning of this inner migration. For they are being called to an exploration of the depths. It is remarkable that the first thing that the prophets attempt to restore to this people that has lost everything is its memory. Memory is the way to the heart: "Remember this ... return to your heart, remember things long past." (Is. 46, 8-9; cf. 44, 21) We are aware today of the crucial importance of this return to the initial experiences and this rediscovery of lost past time for the life of the spirit. Israel must remember. In the prophetic language to remember is to return to the heart; they are one and the same. It's a question of reawakening in ourselves a depth which is one with our truest selves and with our initial vocation. The only help one can get comes from the depths.

This return to authentic being is a difficult undertaking. It must necessarily go through the destruction of the false image that men and women have of themselves. It is first of all lived as a descent into hell. Retracing the history of Israel in a symbolic manner, Ezekiel does not hesitate to re-immerse the latter into its pagan archeology. "By origin and birth you belong to the land of Canaan. Your father was an Amorite and your mother a Hittite. At birth, the very day you were born, there was no one to cut your navel string..."(Ezek. 16, 3-4) The prophet sends

Israel, this overly proud and overly confident people, back to its obscure origins. He reminds them that their essence is not superior to that of others; that it issues from idolatrous tribes; that it is made of the same human stuff and still remains deeply attached to its pagan ancestors: for "there was no one to cut the navel string..." Even more, on the day of its birth no one gave it the most basic care. It was not washed. Abandoned in its own blood, rejected as if from a miscarriage, it was destined to die (Ezek. 16, 4–5).

This is hard language. It destroys all self-complacency. It snatches away the too-flattering image a people had of itself. It brings it back to its primal nakedness; to the essential poverty of the person. It humiliates, however, only to heal. It aims at awakening within the conscience of this people the sense of the gratuity of their existence and their election. Israel owes everything to the sole initiative of God, beginning with its life. It is the one on whom God has had pity:

> I saw you struggling in your blood as I was passing, and I said to you as you lay in your blood: live, and grow like the grass of the fields. You developed, you grew, you reached marriageable age. Your breasts and your hair both grew, but you were quite naked. Then I saw you as I was passing. Your time had come, the time for love. I spread part of my cloak over you and covered your nakedness; I bound myself by oath, I made a covenant with you—it is the Lord Yahweh who speaks—and you became mine. I bathed you in water, I washed the blood off you, I anointed you with oil. I gave you embroidered dresses, fine leather shoes, a linen headband and a cloak of silk. I loaded you with jewels... You grew more

> and more beautiful; and you rose to be queen. The
> fame of your beauty spread through the nations,
> since it was perfect, because I had clothed you with
> my own splendor... But you have become infatuated
> with your own beauty; you have used your fame to
> make yourself a prostitute (Ezek. 16, 6–15).

Once again abandoned and rejected by all, stripped
of all its prerogatives, lost in the immense pagan
world, Israel now must come back in great humility
to its point of departure and renew itself by reaching
this deep part of its being that relies solely on the
pure gratuity of God. In its poverty it is invited to
remember its true identity. to rediscover itself as the
one to whom God has been merciful. Ah! if only Israel could remember!

> Does a virgin forget her ornaments,
> a bride her sash?
> And yet my people have forgotten me,
> for days beyond number... (Jer. 2, 32).

> Does the snow of Lebanon
> vanish from the lofty crag?
> Do the proud waters run dry,
> so coolly flowing?
> And yet my people have forgotten me! (Jer. 18,
>   14–15).

"The virgin," "the bride," "the waters coolly flowing": so many images which evoke a marvelous and
uncontaminated world—the world of beginnings. A
world of dreams far off and pure and yet always
available. A world where fidelity reigns. Snow does
not vanish from the lofty crag. Between it and the
haughty peak there is as if an eternal pact, an inde-
structible covenant. Likewise between the "heart"

and Yahweh. Everything, then, can be reborn with the sparkle of the snows of years gone by. Israel need only rediscover in wonderment the way of its "heart."

"You have never remembered your youth..." (Ezek. 16, 22). This reproach aims at stirring up a forgotten voice from the depths of the soul. It is a call to the depths. It seeks to awaken primal sensitivities:

> For your sake I remember the affection of your
>   youth,
> the love of your bridal days:
> you followed me through the wilderness,
> through a land unsown. (Jer. 2, 1)

The march through the desert, as we know, was not always one of exemplary fidelity. Many missed the food in Egypt and murmured against Moses. And it is indeed in the desert that the people adored the golden calf, thus provoking Yahweh's wrath. But it is not some page from history which is here brought back to memory. The evocation of the bridal days carries another meaning; it is less turned to events of the past then toward certain intimate depths that it aims at awakening.

The lyrical celebration of the past is a symbolic language which permits the person to explore what is most original in himself and thus puts him in contact with hidden sources. There is in each one of us, emerging from the depths of the soul, a remembrance of innocence and of fervor that even the most serious of faults does not succeed in completely effacing. It even happens that this deep memory when it awakens is accompanied by the stunning splendor of our first experiences and is confused with the remembrance of these. But, in reality, it comes from even further back than our deepest memories; it is illumined by another innocence and another splendor. Yes, an Other remembers in us. "For your sake I remember," says Yahweh. This memory of God at the heart of the person is the voice of an always-available unsullied depth and of a reservoir of purity and fervor.

This unexplored domain can only be spoken about in a symbolic manner, in terms of far-off and wonderful remembrances or in the language of a sacred love story. This is how, through the mouths of the prophets, Yahweh's people is invited to return to the ways of its childhood and its youth: ways whose splendor is like that of mornings when the dew is still untouched; ways of wonderment which direct men and women to their hearts.

If only Israel could remember with its heart, remember once more the deep call and the solemn oath, then the covenant would leap out to meet it again like a fresh mountain torrent. Then something would happen. It would rediscover the creative moment. A moment when one can inhale the perfume of Genesis when creation is yet unfinished: the moment of the new heart.

tivity was only beginning. Some felt that he had
gone a little too far. One by the name of Shemaiah of
Nehelam hastened to answer that the man who held
such views should be put in the stocks in an iron
collar. (Jer. 29, 26–28)

Nevertheless, it seemed more and more clear to
everyone that the exile would be a long one and that
they had to organize themselves in consequence. It
does not help to go on lamenting. Life must be
lived. The deportees thus seek to be hired out by the
craftsmen or the merchants of the country. A few
even manage to get into the palace and find places in
public service in the administration.

At the same time that their lot improves, the
exiles mingle more and more with the pagan society.
The latter is not without its attractiveness. The
cities are impressive in their number and in the size
and the beauty of their buildings. The gigantic zig-
gurats of enamaled and mottled bricks, the palaces,
the banks, the temples guarded by lions and winged
bulls, the pools, the gardens—all this worthy of ad-
miration. Nippur, though not Babylon's equal, pro-
vides an image in miniature of the empire and its
enchantment. In the shade of its palm trees the city
watches caravans and ships laden with every imag-
inable product converge on it. Its markets overflow with fruits, spices, precious stones, and silks.
And sometimes in the midst of the noisy crowd of
merchants, the bedecked retinue of an ambassador
makes its way through on the way to Babylon.

And what to say about Babylon, the "pride of the
Chaldeans"? The capital is at its peak. Its authority
extends from the Persian gulf to the hills of Harran

and through Syria as far as Egypt. It eclipses all the
capitals of the Orient with its greatness and splendor. The king Nebuchadnezzar has accumulated his
treasures here. It is here that power, wealth, and
grace meet. Seen from the outside, Babylon looks
like a powerful fortress, the image of the empire it
dominates. Its threefold surrounding walls, twenty
meters wide, serve as base for the countless towers
that reach up to the sky. Eight monumental gates
grant access to the city. The biggest one, the one
through which the royal retinues and liturgical processions pass, is the gate of Ishtar. There begins the
triumphal way to the inner city, a long avenue
paved with cobblestones and bordered by palaces
and temples. The city is built on the two shores of
the Euphrates which are joined by a bridge of five
arches. On the left bank rises the famous temple of
Marduk with its ziggurat a hundred meters high.
Not far away the great palace extends with its
sandstone and basalt terraces which descend by de-
grees down to the river. The wonderful suspended
gardens with their trees emitting the most exotic
scents, their cascades, and the monumental stair-
cases can be found there. From one end of the river
to the other, the wharves are alive with the unload-
ing of all kinds of products and the dealings of a
whole population of merchants.

The fascinating gaze of idols watches over this
display of prosperity and power, an ecstatic and om-
nipresent gaze. It covers and casts a spell over the
entire society. A hypnotic gaze of incredible sugges-
tive power. These idols with their enormous eyes
and with their heads sunken into their shoulders—

heritages of Sumerian religion—are not the images of any creature; in their own way they are a language of the sacred. They symbolize the primordial forces. They place the whole activity of men and women in relationship with these powers; they integrate them into the great poem of creation in the cosmic order which Marduk symbolizes. On certain days of the year these idols are paraded in the city on the backs of men with great pomp and circumstance. The most solemn moment of the city's religious life occurs on the New Year during the Spring equinox. Then the gods of all the great cities of the empire come to Babylon to visit Marduk, the god of gods. Male and female dancers process slowly amidst shouts and the clapping of hands. The Poem of Creation is recited; an entire people celebrates the renewal of the eternal victory of Marduk.

The deportees from Judah do not escape the fascination exercised by this society into which they have been plunged. The power that is displayed before their eyes and that seems to be rooted in the eternal is indeed of a nature to disturb them. It raises certain anguishing questions for them. The name of Yahweh has always been synonymous with power for them. Isn't Yahweh the almighty? Isn't this how he made himself known to their fathers and how they themselves learned to know him?

> God, we have heard with our own ears,
> our ancestors have told us
> of the deeds you performed in their days,
> in days long ago, by your hand.
>
> To put them in the land you dispossessed the
> nations,

you harried the peoples to make room for them;
it was not by their swords they won the land,
it was not by their arms they gained the victory:
it was your right hand, your arm
and the light of your face—because you loved them.

You it was, my king, my God,
who won those victories for Jacob (Ps. 44, 1-4).

This is what they have always been taught. Hasn't
the history of their people from Abraham to Solomon
been one of a long ascent to power under the leader-
ship of Yahweh, the almighty? In truth there have
been nine centuries of successive growth and in-
crease in power. The patriarchs had already been
the recipients of an overabundance of goods.
Yahweh had mulitplied their children, their flocks,
and their length of days. Then when Israel fell into
slavery in Egypt, he freed them with "a mighty hand
and an outstretched arm" and enriched it with the
spoils of Egypt. He made a people out of them and
chased away all other peoples. He gave them a land
where milk and honey flowed. Israel established itself, developed, and prospered in it. It became
strong. And one day it attained the level of a kingdom. Its renown then spread among the nations.
Jerusalem, its capital, was equal in influence and
splendor to the capitals of neighboring countries.
What a long way it had come from Abraham the
nomadic shepherd! This slow, continual ascent to
power and glory reached its peak during the reign of
Solomon. The temple was built then. In its size, its
wealth, and its splendor it was the symobl of all the
power and the glory that Yahweh and given to his

people. It was truly the tangible sign of the presence of the almighty in the midst of his people.

"Yahweh brought Solomon's greatness to its height in the sight of all Israel, and gave him a reign of such splendor as none that had reigned over Israel before him had ever known" (I Chron. 29, 25).

What is left of this power today? Nothing at all. Everything is destroyed. The nation has fallen into desolation. Yahweh's people has become the weakest, the most wretched of all peoples. Where is Yahweh in this debacle? What is he doing? Where is his all-powerfulness? The deportees from Judah wonder to themselves.

Certainly they have sinned. They acknowledge it. At least the best of them do. They lacked trust in Yahweh by aligning themselves with other nations and other gods and by wanting to run their own affairs by themselves. But have they sinned more than their fathers whom Yahweh had always been quick to forgive?

Why then this harsh treatment? Why this unprecedented devastation? And above all why this endless silence? Before, when the people strayed Yahweh punished them but quickly forgave them in order not to provoke the pagan nations into arrogance: "In you our fathers put their trust, they trusted and you rescued them: they called to you for help and they were saved, they never trusted you in vain" (Ps. 22, 5–6). This forgiveness was manifested by a return to prosperity and power. It is just such a return that the deportees would like to see happen. They wait and watch for a sign of power. But the years slip by and still no sign is given. If only they could see the beginning of something. But there is nothing. Why this abandonment? Oh, what a strange silence into which God has withdrawn himself!

It is nighttime in the soul of Israel. "Days of mist and darkness," it is written in the book of Ezekiel the prophet (Ezek. 34, 12). If only the exiles could celebrate their liturgy, offer sacrifices to Yahweh, organize solemn processions in his honor! Through the ancient rites and the splendors of the liturgy, they could catch their breath and find some assurance. But even this is denied them. There is no longer any altar or sacrifice.

"Where is Yahweh, your God?" the pagans mockingly ask them. But in the deepest part of themselves, the deportees anguishingly ask themselves the same question. Is Yahweh's silence a sign of his powerlessness? Would Yahweh have been conquered along with this people? Is he really the Almighty? Is he the Only One? Or else is he only one god among others and perhaps even a god less powerful than the others? The soul of Israel is plunged into a night similar to the primal chaos. The exiles have lost many things in this torment. They have lost their nation, native land, and their possessions; they have also lost their close relatives and their friends. But there is worse than this: they have lost their God.

"Where is Yahweh?" This is the question they are raising. But none of them are yet asking: "Who is Yahweh?" The silence of God simply means for them that God no longer corresponds to the idea of him that was given to them, to the signs of his presence they have received. None of them says in his heart: "I do not know Yahweh, I do not know his ways." They are all so sure of knowing him that they think they know him as if they had grown up together! Israel has lost its God but it has not yet discovered itself to be poor before Yahweh, poor in its knowledge of him. It murmurs: " . . . and when I call and shout, he shuts out my prayer. He had blocked my ways with cut stones" (Lam. 3, 8–9). Israel does not yet know that these stones are only the mirror of its own heart.

Chapter 6

Midnight Crossing

The years have slipped by. Much water has flowed over the plain and many illusions have vanished from the hearts of the deportees. Some of them have lost all hope of returning to their native land. Others have died and have been buried in pagan territory. Children, on the other hand, have been born. But their birth has hardly been a cause for celebration.

Nevertheless, the situation of the exiles has considerably improved with time. Following Jeremiah's advice, they have built and planted. The cleverest ones have become successful businessmen. Some are even on the brink of acquiring a fortune; they live in stylish villas, enjoy an extensive social life, and are served by hundreds of slaves. On the Middle-Euphrates, in the canton of Nippur, the Israelite towns are prospering. And wealth is accompanied by increasing power and influence. In Babylon, the sons of Jacob now have access to the imperial court. The successor of Nebuchadnezzar openly declares his friendship toward them.

41

The life of the Jewish colony could easily have accommodated itself to this affluence. History then would have nothing to tell of the exile apart from reports of bank accounts such as those of the Murashu bank which had numerous Israelite clients. But for some of the deportees the exile has taken on another dimension; it has been transformed into the highest of spiritual adventures. If these men and women no longer suffer materially, the fact remains that they are profoundly dissatisfied. And all the wealth of the Fertile Crescent could not satisfy them. They await something else. The prophet Ezekiel had told them: "make yourselves a new heart." These words have finally resounded deeply enough in them. Now they long for this renewal.

To create a new heart does not simply entail changing one's way of seeing, feeling, thinking, and wanting. A much more radical move is at stake. It has to do with rediscovering the vital forces of life and creative enthusiasm. It has to do with returning to the wellsprings of life or, in a word, with being reborn.

How can these men and women be reborn? How can uprooted beings be replanted in the earth and from its nourishment rediscover enthusiasm for life when the very soil itself is lacking? These men and women are fully aware that they are no longer a power in the world. They have no illusion about this, especially the poorest and humblest among them. Nevertheless, they have not for all that renounced their hope in the promised land. Nor their hope for greatness. Their hearts reject such an abandonment. And they have learned to listen to their hearts.

Obscurely, but invincibly, they feel called to great accomplishments. Within the deepest parts of themselves a force pushes off all temptation that might lead to decline and obliteration. This mysterious force emerging from the deepest parts of their history obliges them to look toward the future.

At night when all noises have subsided, these men and women recollect themselves religiously. Around them the entire empire is asleep. Night takes possession of the land. But up above in a pure and unveiled sky thousands of stars light up. And such incredible stars! Then these men and women of Judah remember: "Look up to heaven and count the stars if you can.Such will be your descendants" (Gen. 15, 5). The immense promise awakens them, stirs their memory, challenges them, and sets before them the true dimension of their destiny. They are promised to greatness: "I will make you a great nation . . . all the tribes of the earth shall bless themselves by you . . ." (Gen. 12, 2-3). "You shall become the father of a multitude of nations . . ." (Gen. 17, 4). Are they not sons and daughters of this promise? They have no doubts about it. They are not only its sons and daughters but also its heirs. They are the ones meant to harvest this heritage today. It is upon them that the future of the promise rests. On their faith and nothing else. What a responsibility! If they try to evade it the greatness of Israel and the blessing of the nations will be lost forever.

But how can this promise still be believed in? In the present situation, it looks like a joke. What is left of a "great people" is a small remnant scattered among the nations. This is what they have become in reality! Everything lends itself to skepticism and denial: their small number, their powerlessness, and the flatly opportunistic attitude of many of them now well established during their exile like a herd of young calves in a rich pasture. Try to speak to them of the promised land and its greatness. Do they have any other expectations? None whatsoever. Above all not a new heart. But this is still not the worst.

The worst consists in a feeling of unworthiness which surreptitiously slips its way into the soul dripping its venom and leaving a poisoned conscience. Repeated infidelities were indeed what chased them away from the promised land. They have so soiled this land that it ended up by vomiting them. And now, as once before, Yahweh has placed his angel with his sword of fire before the gate of the Garden of Eden to forbid access to it. It is useless to think that one can get in. The road is blocked. There is no trespassing in the kingdom. On certain days, the awareness of their unworthiness weighs so heavily and so cruelly taht it completely clouds their horizon and rises up on their way like an inaccessible mountain. It is then that Jacob's ancient struggle for the sons and daughters of Israel is renewed.

Jacob had also experienced being brutally forbidden access to the promised land at the very moment that he was getting ready to enter it after twenty years of exile. He had reached the border without mishap and was about to cross at Jabbok. His two wives, his children, his servants, and his flock had already crossed the torrent. He had remained on the opposite shore. Night had fallen; Jacob wanted to cross alone. Alone with his thoughts of the return.

Then suddenly someone leapt at him from out of the shadows. Jacob immediately became aware of the extent of the danger. He was defenseless. No one was around to rescue him. And he had nothing to offer in exchange for his life. All that he owned lay on the other side of the torrent. He was alone and poor as on the day of his death. There was only one way out and that was to run.

But Jacob would not run nor turn his back; rather, he was going to face it. No matter what happened! Jacob was bare-handed but he had the promise on his side. The Lord Yahweh had promised him this land and committed himself to one day bringing him back to his own country: "I will give to you and your descendants the land on which are are lying. Your descendants shall be like the specks of dust on the ground; you shall spread to the West and the East, to the North and the South, and all the tribes of the earth shall bless themselves by you and your descendants. Be sure that I am with you; I will keep you safe wherever you go, and bring you back to this land..." (Gen. 28, 13–15). There is no one in the whole wide world that could prevail against this promise. So then, mustering all the strength of his faith, Jacob resisted. He held back the first assault, then the second.

After a moment of this hand-to-hand combat had elapsed, having closely felt out his adversary, Jacob felt at the bottom of his strength and in the deepest part of his soul that he was dealing with a superhuman power. He was not fighting against a mere man but against the almighty himself.

What could he do against this force which can

make one live or die? What merit could he bring to bear? At this instant, Jacob saw himself naked before the living God. No doubt it would have been better to give up the struggle and fall on one's knees.

Jacob rejected this temptation. Assuredly, there was no merit which he could claim. But God had promised. And Jacob clung to this promise. It was his weapon and he would not let go of it. He continued to fight and to fight ferociously. He fought for this land and the great destiny which had been promised him. He fought for his descendants and for all the nations of the earth which would be blessed by him. He fought for the future of the world. He had never felt himself so poor and so free. Marvelously free. And the more he saw himself stripped of everything, clinging to the promise alone, the more he experienced his strength growing.

And the hours of the night slipped by without the Other conquering. The latter, seeing that he could not master him, struck him a sharp blow on the hip joint. Jacob quivered all over. His hip was dislocated. But he didn't let go of his hold. And then the first rays of dawn lightened the horizon. And the unknown one said to Jacob: "Let me go, for day is breaking." But Jacob answered: "I will not let you go unless you bless me"(Gen. 32, 27). These words—the first ones of the entire night—transfigured a struggle unto death into one of love, into one of mutual recognition. God acknowledged that he could no longer disengage himself: he is bound by his promise, conquered by it; and he accepts this. He then said to Jacob: "Your name shall no longer be Jacob, but Israel, 'the conqueror of God'" (Gen. 32, 29).

Jacob, for his part, would have liked to have known the name of his adversary: "I beg you, tell me your name" (Gen. 32, 30). But God remains God. He would not tell him his name. He only blessed Jacob and no more. Then in the bright splendor of morning, Jacob, limping and glowing with divine blessings, crossed the torrent foaming at his feet. At once conqueror and cripple, he entered the promised land. This is how Jacob tipped the scales of the destiny of the world in favor of the kingdom. "Because I have seen God face to face," he said. "and I have survived" (Gen. 32, 31).

Today in the night of the exile, the sons of Israel, the descendants of the "Conqueror of God," have to sustain the same struggle. They are to undergo the same solitude, the same agony and the same startling experience. And with the same weapon, too: the promise. The latter may seem very fragile and derisory. But isn't this what it seemed to be for the patriarchs themselves? Didn't it come off as a big joke for Abraham? He was a hundred years old with no children and his body was a wreck. And the womb of Sarah his wife was likewise dead. Humanly speaking, the promise defied common sense from the start. Sarah, moreover, when she first heard it could not help but laugh. Only Abraham believed. He believed against all hope with all the seriousness and naiveté of someone with a new heart. He believed in "the God who brings the dead to life and calls into being what does not exist" (Rom. 4, 17).

It is to such a faith that the exiles are called. Until now they have relied on their own strength and on military and political alliances. They sought for greatness where it could not be found; they brought it down to the level of their mediocre ambitions. They were then in danger of death. But now among some of them a new language is heard: "The person overcome with an affliction, who goes his way bowed down and frail, with failing eyes and hungering soul, he is the one to give you glory, Lord, and due observance. We do not rely on the merits of our ancestors and of our kings to offer you our humble plea, Lord our God . . ." (Baruch 2, 18–19). Those who speak in this way do not seek to recreate their personage by leaning on the merits of their ancestors or their own personal merits. They receive the advice of no one, nor do they recommend themselves. The ear of grain that they thought contained only good seed was but chaff and wind. They know it and accept it. They have become poor before God. But they believe, as did Abraham, in the God who brings the dead to life and calls into being what does not exist. They believe in the God of the promise. And there is nothing that can withstand this faith. Not even the memory of their sins and the feeling of their unworthiness. They have swept all this away. Only the splendor of the promise remains.

For these men and women, the exile has ceased being a misfortune and a malediction. It has become the site where the human being, in the depths of his or her night, has to deal with the living God.

The midnight hour has struck. The day is still far off. But this is where the other side of night begins.

They express the deepest as well as the most heart-wrenching experience that men and women can have of the transcendence of God. They proclaim that there is nothing that can restrain Yahweh: not the temple, not Jerusalem, not the kingdom, not the land. All these can crumble and disappear. What remains is this incomparable reality: Yahweh reigns.

These words possess infinite greatness. We must not conclude too quickly that we have understood them. What they affirm is not self-evident. They even contradict, at first glance, Israel's deepest faith. In fact, for the people of the Bible, "it is here below, on earth, that the religious destiny of men and women is fully worked out. For the here-below is not only the sojourning place of men and women; it is also the dwelling place of God" (André Neher, *Moîse et al vocation juive.* Paris, 1956, p. 175).

Nothing is more foreign to the religious experience of Israel than the notion of a God living apart and withdrawn in a supraterrestrial and intemporal existence. Waking up after a night spent out in the open, Jacob cries out: "Truly, Yahweh is in this place and I never knew it" (Gen. 28, 16). This is a basic and permanent given of the faith of Israel: The glory of Yahweh is on earth. It is present not in the manner of pagan divinities that manifest themselves in cosmic and vital forces, but as binding itself to a people and its history. God says to Jacob: "I am Yahweh. the God of your ancestor Abraham and the God of Isaac" (Gen. 28, 13), "I am with you." (Gen. 28, 15). Not only as the one who lives close to men and women in general but as the one who is close to such and such a man or woman in particular (Ex. 3, 15). He has bound himself to individual beings, their history, and their destiny to the extent that in the thought of Israel Yahweh is inconceivable without his people. Without them he is no longer Yahweh. For Israel to know Yahweh does not entail discovering the mysteries and secrets of the divine essence, but rather experiencing a presence: an active presence on earth within a precise human history; a presence which manifests itself before all else as a liberating power: "I am Yahweh your God who brought you out of the land of Egypt, out of the house of slavery ..." (Deut. 5, 6; cf. Ex. 20, 2). "Yahweh your God is among you, a God who is great and terrible" (Deut. 7, 21). It is impossible, therefore, to separate, faith in Yahweh from faith in his presence to his people.

Such a faith, far from drawing men and women to solitary and temporal contemplation of the divine essence, leads them to action in the world. It impells them to face the historical moment and find their nourishment in events. The exodus was such an event carved from the heart of history. It was a physical, social, and political as well as a religious event, a liberation of the body as well as of the soul. And the long journeying in the desert was in no way a quest for solitude wherein men and women would have chosen to establish themselves outside of time in the peace of contemplation. Quite to the contrary, the desert was a place where Israel prepared itself to courageously assume its worldly destiny; it was the crucible out of which an original people with its own laws and its own particular historical vocation was formed. It was there that an indissoluble bond between the eternal and historical time was established in the consciousness of Israel.

Strengthened by this awareness, Israel set forth to conquer the promised land. It drove away everyone in its path. It occupied the land, planted, built, and governed. It gave itself completely to its human adventure, at once divine and earthly, with increasing success and boldness. And one day, with the help of Yahweh, it attained the level of a kingdom: "I put a beautiful diadem on your head" (Ezek. 16, 12). At this point the people of Yahweh began to reign. And Yahweh reigned on earth through his people.

This desire to act in the world with the power of Yahweh affirms itself throughout the history of Israel. It can even be found when Israel goes astray. And it is precisely in reference to this desire for earthly efficacy that the words quoted previously can take on their full meaning: "The garland has fallen from our heads ...." These words are the expression of a deep and total failure. They ascertain the end of everything that a people had unceasingly pursued. The bells toll for hope and for a *raison d'etre*. For such a failure is not only grievously felt; it can only be lived as a scandal. What it brings to the surface is that Yahweh is not present to his people in the way they thought he was. In the great misfortune which fell upon Israel, at no time did Yahweh intervene to prevent the irreparable. He allowed events to unfold according to their own fateful dynamism. He abandoned his people to shame and defeat. In a word, he was the great absent one. The logical conclusion of all this would then be: "Our reign is over, but also that of Yahweh."

But suddenly from the deepest level of its despair, Israel's religious consciousness rebounds and cries

out its faith: "The garland has fallen from our heads
... But you, Yahweh, you remain forever, your reign
endures from age to age." Which amounts to saying:
"Your reign is not held in check by our failures; it is
not bound to our human vicissitudes; indeed, there is
nothing to which it is bound. It continues and even
affirms itself through the devastation that is ours."

To acknowledge this is to allow oneself to be taken
up by the sheer grandeur of God. Yahweh is not to be
numbered among his creatures; even when he mul-
tiplies his covenants with them, he is not on the
same level as they are; he always remains the Only
One. And face to face with the sheer grandeur of
God, men and women are to be silent and adore.

Is this to say that Israel thus renounces its deepest
intuition, namely, that of the presence of God in history, in order to find its refuge in a transcendence
cut off from the world? Would it thus betray its vocation which is to unite the eternal with historical
time, in order to turn to a God who reigns above
history? Certainly not. The acknowledgement of the
reign of Yahweh even in the midst of the devastation
of his people has a completely different meaning. For
Israel, Yahweh is and remains the God present to
history, and this in a sovereign way. He is the master of history. But what the exiles began to catch a
glimpse of in the light of the exile experience is that
the reign of Yahweh does not allow itself to be as-
similated to a political power; it is of a different
order of greatness and its ways are mysterious. This
reign is inseparable from the very mystery of God;
he is the beyond at the heart of history.

Chapter 8

A Broken-Hearted People

To return to the living God is to rediscover the God of mystery. In spite of the ruins accumulated over his people, Yahweh reigns. But there is no sign of this reign left. The night is total. "We have at this time no leader, no prophet, no prince, no holocaust, no sacrifice, no oblation, no incense, no place where we can offer you the first-fruits and win your favor..." (Dan. 3, 38–39).

And then, at this very point, the song of the poor arises in the night; "... But may the contrite soul, the humbled spirit be acceptable to you... such let our sacrifice be to you today..." (Dan. 3, 39–40). "Sacrifice gives you no pleasure, were I to offer holocaust, you would not have it. My sacrifice is this broken spirit, you will not scorn this crushed and broken heart" (Ps. 51, 16–17). At the heart of this prayer a certitude is being born, a light filters through. But it is much more than simply a certitude or a ray of light. What takes place is an unparalleled encounter.

The God who is above and beyond all things, who is bound to nothing, not the temple, Jerusalem, the land, nor any institution, now reveals himself as the one who is close to the "broken-hearted," mysteriously present to them.This truth which the Bible asserts in many places ("Yahweh is close to the broken-hearted") bursts forth from the ordeal of the exile. Such is the overwhelming experience of these men and women who have accepted to enter into the night of God.

We hear an echo of this experience in the words the prophet Isaiah puts into the mouth of Yahweh:

> For thus speaks the Most High,
> whose home is in eternity,
> whose name is holy:
> "I live in a high and holy place,
> but I am also with the contrite and humbled spirit,
> to give the humbled spirit new life,
> to revive the broken-hearted" (Is. 57, 15).

The high and holy place where the Most High dwells is his own mystery, his holy and impenetrable being. This dwelling place is the only appropriate one, the only one worthy of him. No one can pretend to lift himself up to this eternal dwelling place and cross its threshold. But the God who is inaccessible lets it be known that between himself and the "broken-hearted" all distances are abolished. The one who is infinitely above is also mysteriously "with." Yahweh dwells in the "broken–hearted":

> Thus says Yahweh:
> With heaven my throne
> and earth my footstool,
> what house could you build me,
> what place could you make for my rest?

All of this was made by my hand
and all of this is mine—it is Yahweh who speaks.
But my eyes are drawn to the man
of humbled and contrite spirit, with a poor and
   broken heart,
who trembles at my word (Is. 66, 1–2).

These words are not only meant to console. They express a truth which can only be discovered through an experience of devastation and which is of deepest concern for the revelation of the living God. The mystery of God is also that of his nearness. There is a profound and essential bond between the revelation of God in the world and the experience which the Bible designates by the simple words: "the broken-hearted." The revelation of the living God happens by way of this experience.

To speak of the "broken-hearted" as the place of preference for the revelation of God is not to get wrapped up in subjectivity. When the Bible speaks of "heart" in this way, it has no intention of exalting religious sentimentality. There is no romantic feeling which can adequately translate the biblical experience of the "broken-heart." Nor any pietistic fervor. It is something completely different.

The "heart" in biblical language designates the deepest reality of the person, in opposition to mere appearance or falsehood. The "heart" is the hidden source of our primal and secret energies: "More than all else, keep watch over your heart, since here are the wellsprings of life" (Pr. 4, 23). Freudian psychology places "Eros" at the center and at the root of our psychic being. The Bible likewise. But for the latter, this fundamental power of love cannot be reduced to aggressive and possessive desire. This is not what it

is, primarily. There is in man and woman, above all
else, a loving power that binds them to the mystery
of being. The "heart" contains a primal power of
communion with everything that exists. Because of
this, it has fathomless depths which one cannot
plumb and which make it akin to the creator's power
of love itself. It is through the "heart" that men and
women are created in the image of God. Far from
closing up men and women within themselves, the
energies which dwell in their "hearts" give them the
impetus to go to others; they open them up to the
highest manifestations of kindness and, through
this, to God. It is significant that for the prophets, to
return to the "heart" and to return to God are one
and the same undertaking. By getting back in touch
with their hearts, men and women rediscover the
deepest dimension of their being, the one that puts
them in touch again with the living God.

But men and women can turn their hearts away
from their initial orientation. "The heart," writes
Pascal, "loves the universal being naturally, and itself naturally, according to its obedience to either;
and it hardens against one or the other, as it
pleases..." (*Pascal's Pensees*, N.Y., 1950, p. 343).
Therein lies the drama. Men and women can choose
themselves in an absolute and exclusive way. They
can then set themselves up as centers of the world,
reducing everything to the level of their desires and
ambitions. By so doing, they close themselves not
only to others but to their own depths: that holy and
private part of their being that links them with the
mystery of being and with God himself. The "heart"
hardens itself; it becomes a well of dark shadows.

These are idolatrous times. And idolatrous times are always times of exile. Men and women are living far from their true being and deep roots. They no longer inhabit their "hearts." They wander in a foreign land, at the service of alien gods (Jer. 5, 19). They have become empty of their own substance. The most profound words on this state of alienation have been uttered by the prophet Jeremiah: "Vanity they pursued, vanity they became"(Jer. 2, 5).

One can thus understand how for the prophets to return to Yahweh and to return to one's "heart" represent one and the same process. Men and women can exist and truly find themselves only in the movement which opens them to the One who is. They are at home only in this openness. This is where they can acquire their full stature. Only here can they breathe their native air.

But this return to the "heart" does not take place without some kind of experience of brokenness. The small world within which men and women have closed themselves must be shattered. No matter where the sharp blows come from. A breach is finally made through our walls. Our securities are suddenly taken away from us and we are left with the total and brute reality. "The city is taken," the temple destroyed. This is where the experience of the "broken heart" begins. It is first of all experienced as a great void. Men and women can no longer find anything to hold on to. There is no solid ground to stand on. Only the raging seas and the night. "My heart is broken within me," cries out Jeremiah, "I am like a drunken man, a man overcome with wine—because of Yahweh and his holy words"(Jer. 23, 9).

This devastation throws the soul into deep anguish. But this is still only the first aspect of the experience of the "broken heart." Yahweh says: "I will bring distress on them, to see if they will find me then" (Jer. 10, 18). The "broken heart" exposes itself to the tempest; it consents to being stripped of everything which sheltered it and to losing all its footholds. It accepts the collapse of the religious world it was accustomed to. It can no longer anticipate who God is or what are his ways. It does not say, "God is dead," but simply, "I do not know him yet." This acknowledgement of one's poverty and unknowing leads it to great adoration. The "broken heart" lets God be God. What seemed to be an abyss of desolation becomes a place of preference where men and women are once again taken up by the mystery of God.

This new relationship which is established at the deepest part of one's existence does not, nonetheless, destroy one's basic solitude. If in this experience men and women allow God to be God, God, for his part, allows men and women to be themselves. He does not intervene in their favor; he does not get them out of trouble; he does not guarantee them any power or happiness. He remains truly with them only in abandoning them to their solitude and their night.

But then what can the following words really mean: "Yahweh is close to the broken-hearted"?

What can be perceived of God in this experience is paradoxically, first of all, his infinite distance, his transcendence: "Yes, the heavens are as high above earth as my ways are above your ways, my thoughts above your thoughts" (Is. 55, 9). The "broken-hearted" measure the entire distance separating them from God. They do so through the painful awareness of their sin and the sincere avowal of their wrongdoing. They have a contrite heart. Nevertheless, this painful awareness is not what comes first, but rather is the consequence of something much deeper; it is a reflection of the heart-rending perception of the holiness of God and of his infinite innocence. The experience of the "broken-hearted" is first of all that of a heart dazzled by the holiness of God. Dazzled and wounded. "What a wretched state I am in! I am lost, for I am a man of unclean lips"(Is. 6, 5). At the beginning, there is the radiance of the holiness of God in the soul. And, as a kind of aftershock, the sin and misery of men and women are fully displayed. Confronted, then, by this twofold revelation of the holiness of God and of its own sinfulness, the soul is shaken by both: a tremor of love and one of horror. The heart breaks itself.

This, however, is not where the experience of the "broken heart" stops. At the deepest level of the mystery of God, as he is revealed here, there is the concern for the lost soul and the pathetic movement of the holy God toward sinful men and women. Yahweh does not rejoice over the death of sinners. Quite to the contrary, he too wants them alive, saved and made holy: "You will not scorn this crushed and broken heart" (Ps. 51, 17).To his exiled people whom he compares to an abandoned spouse, Yahweh declares: "I did forsake you for a brief moment, but with great love will I take you back. In excess of anger, for a moment I hid my face from you. But

with everlasting love I have taken pity on you..."
(Is. 54, 7–8).

Thus, for the "broken-hearted" the holy and deep emotion, the sacred tremor, are not primarily to be found in men and women. These are in God himself in his concern for the lost which inclines him to communicate with them. The "broken-hearted" discover the living God. The life of God in biblical understanding cannot be reduced to something rational. It doesn't let itself be rationalized or moralized. Yahweh is the living one par excellence. In no way is he an abstract principle. In him deep emotions are at work: creative emotion and that which inclines him towards the lost: the great mercy of God. Yahweh, to be sure, is spirit. But his spirit is passionate.

This God has nothing olympian about him. He does not hover over men and women and their histories in serene indifference. His is a state of concern for them. He is the beyond at the very heart of the most humble, the most degreeded human existence. He is so as a liberating power, as a call to renewal, a source of dreams and creativity and also as an unrest and a wound. This is how he is present to the "broken-hearted."

The "broken heart" is the breach through which something new can still take place. It is an openness to the living and unpredictable God: the God who comes.

How many of the deportees went through this experience? It is difficult to say. Pioneers are always few in number. There are some adventures which can only be undertaken well in solitude. Pascal wrote, "I love these adorers unknown to the world and even to the prophets."

But it can happen that these unknown adorers can also have a prophet who speaks in their name. Isn't the great vision related by the prophet Ezekiel a very colorful and symbolic expression of what is in the process of being revealed in the night to the heart of Israel? Walking one day along the banks of the river, Ezekiel sees the glory of Yahweh in all its power coming toward him in the shape of a stormy wind (Ezek. 1, 1–28). The same glory that the prophet Isaiah had once contemplated in the temple of Jerusalem in the midst of liturgical festivities is now unleashing itself here in exile, under an open sky and in pagan territory far from the temple and Jerusalem! And with what fury and freedom! It comes and goes, as it wishes, completely unbridled. Four fantastic beings are harnessed to its chariot and these represent all the forces of creation as well as symbolize the great Babylonian divinities. Yahweh reigns and he is unrivaled. He is the unique one. His glory clearly knows no boundaries. It is at home everywhere. Nothing binds it. But it is to be found where men and women journey humbly, far from their native land, in the "broken-hearted." It allows itself to be met in the midst of the storm. This is how Yahweh dwells in the "broken-hearted": as in a storm.

Chapter 9

The Storms of Life

Nothing could better symbolize the extent of the devastation of a "broken heart" than this valley in the midst of which the prophet Ezekiel finds himself brought by the hand of Yahweh (Ezek. 37, 1ff.). The prophet can roam all over the valley. Not a soul is alive. Everywhere he trips over dismembered skeletons. Dry bones lie spread on the ground as far as the eye can see. A desolate scene, to be sure, but one also open to the advent of the spirit. There is no resistance left, no stiffness. But also no limits. Men and women find themselves once again at one with the primal earth. They have again become like a "son of man": mortals. Like Abraham, they can now believe in the God who makes the dead come to life.

Henceforth, there is nothing left to stop the spirit. The latter can blow fully from all the four winds. The power of renewal can unleash itself. "Prophesy to the breath; prophesy, son of man. Say to the breath, 'The Lord Yahweh says this: Come from the four winds, breath; breathe on these dead; let them live!'" (Ezek. 37, 9). The prophet repeats what he was been told and it echoes throughout the valley. And the storms of life subside. One can hear throughout the valley the motion of bones clattering against one another, each one seeking its proper joint. And behold the dead now stand on their feet! They are alive, all of them! A great and immense army (Ezek. 37, 10).

When the human spirit is grappling with such experiences, time is needed to grasp their deep meaning. "...These bones are the whole House of Israel...The Lord Yahweh says this: I am now going to open your graves; I mean to raise you from your graves, my people. And I shall put my spirit in you, and you will love..." (Ezek. 37, 11–14). Gradually, the mind of the prophet sees the light. The true prophetic dimension of the vision unfolds. Ezekiel understands that what is going on in symbolic language is a deep renewal in the hearts of men and women. He enters within the interior meaning of the vision. And he can hear Yahweh tell him: "I shall give you a new heart, and put a new spirit in you; I shall remove the heart of stone from your bodies and give you a heart of flesh instead. I shall put my spirit in you...." (Ezek. 36, 26–27; cf. 11, 19)

We have come a long way! Not that long ago, in the name of Yahweh, Ezekiel had told his companions in exile: "Make yourselves a new heart and a new spirit." (Ezek. 18, 31). It was easy to say. But how to make it happen? And what can a new heart and a new spirit mean? And now we see Yahweh himself taking the initiative for the renewal of his creatures. A wonderful metamorphosis takes place. The heart of stone which we carry in us and to which we have become so accustomed that we can no longer estimate the extent of its hardness, he will remove and put a heart of flesh in its place. For such will be the new heart: a heart of flesh. As for the new spirit, it will be the spirit of Yahweh himself which will be at the heart of the creature: "I shall put my spirit in you."

What is most astonishing and most wonderful in this renewal of men and women is that the spirit of Yahweh finds itself intimately associated with the heart of flesh. One does not go without the other: one is given with the other. The highest and most pure spiritual experience is also the one which restores to men and women their deep and true carnality. Participation with the spirit of God is linked to this deepening which enables them to rediscover the living waters of tenderness and communion in the most intimate part of themselves. To open oneself to the passionate spirit of Yahweh, therefore, also means to be born into one's full and deep humanity. When men and women allow themselves to be seized by the spirit, the latter never ceases its activity until it has penetrated and touched the most obscure parts of their roots; and there, it recreates "the ancient, forgotten Eden of tenderness."

One knows only too well how life with its struggles for priorities, its ambitions, its fears, and its desire to succeed and dominate can harden hearts and allow aggression and resentment to accumulate within. The primal powers of wonderment and communion are quickly stifled. And the worst hardening is not that of one's feelings. It is rather the steely, cold, and withering harshness of intelligence; the harshness of a mediocre and abstract mind which in the name of truth is unaware and devoid of feeling. The heart of the one who has no heart. This is what hardness of heart means.

God knows what a heavy stone men and women can carry within their breasts! A stone under which the deep layers of the soul lie buried. The rock must be broken for the living waters to flow anew. Only the "broken-hearted" who have allowed themselves to be dispossessed of their self-sufficiency and their will to power by the action of the spirit can rediscover their hidden sources. And it is the spirit which moves them to rediscover these sources. The spirit of Yahweh needs every fiber of our hearts in order to be born within us. This part of ourselves that we thought to be forever destroyed, the spirit calls forth to life a second time. With it we are born anew; we are new creatures opened up to communion with all that is.

Reconciling purity and tenderness, innocence and fervor, is not the least new dimension of this heart of flesh. François Mauriac asked, 'Why have purity and tenderness been separated?" The pure being—or the one who wishes to be so—is often hard and haughty as if men and women had to choose between a purity which renders them cold as ice and a love which devours them by degrading them. But now the same divine word promises to the exiled both a heart of flesh and a purity comparable to the transparency of flowing springs: "I shall pour out clean water over you and you will be cleansed" (Ezek. 36,

25). Purified—but not disincarnated. In the heart of flesh recreated by the breath of Yahweh everything has its being and is rediscovered as limpid and luminous. Everything, even Eros.

This pure water which penetrates the heart and frees it from its heaviness and its impurities is not to be confused with the waters of legal purifications. It is rather the water "humble, precious, and chaste" of which Francis of Assisi sang. It is an intimate and primal reality. Inseparable from the breath of the spirit, it carries the seeds of life.

Water and spirit! Isn't this the primordial pair that serves as the prelude to all of creation at the beginning of Genesis? "In the beginning ... God's spirit hovered over the water" (Gen. 1, 1). When spirit and water unite, a new world is being born. The night of exile becomes the night of great beginnings. A night for nativity.

Chapter 10

The Source and the River

A new heart can never be a permanent acquisition. It is a reality which is always being born and always being threatened. The weight of old habits, of group pressure, and of its own past history is still alive. Invincibly, men and women seek to reconstruct their lost paradise and to return to their former limits within which they felt so strongly protected. And even those who have entered the spiritual light of the presence can still look backwards.

And so in his exile Ezekiel dreams, on certain days, of a reconstructed temple. He sees it, describes it, measures its length, heighth, and width. Complacently and admiringly. He who had contemplated on the banks of the river the glory of Yahweh moving freely under the open sky in the midst of the pagan nations and had seen it come near to the "brokenhearted," now on his return witnesses a vision in the reconstructed temple. And, ecstatic, he sees the glory of Yahweh confined once again to a building

71

made of stone. As if the exile had only been a paren-
thesis and everything could go back to what it was
in the past!

We are both astonished and ill at ease before this
vision of the future developed in the last chapters of
the book of Ezekiel. Isn't this temple made of stone
and set at the center of the restored Jerusalem the
negation, the veritable tombstone, of what had so
slowly and with so many tears finally seen the light
of day during the night of exile? The spirit seems to
have ceased breathing. The storm has ended. But,
with it, creative lyricism. A lengthy and detailed de-
scription where everything is calculated and measured now takes its place. We are spared no detail.
The poet is replaced by the geometrist, the prophet
by the organizer and calculator.

What is even more serious is that considerations
about the new heart fade away and are replaced by
prescriptions of legal purity. Everything reverts to
its old patterns. In this way men and women always
wind up putting new wine into old wine skins. Job,
too, once he had been stripped of all that he had, also
found himself once again surrounded by his many
camels and donkeys (Job 62, 12).

But is this really a step backwards? Men and
women undergo some experiences which have a last-
ing influence. Those who have struggled with God
all night long finally to be blessed by him can indeed
resume their journey in the company of their flocks
when the sun rises. They no longer move at the same
pace, it is true: from now on they limp (Gen. 32, 32).
And even if they seem to settle in their past once

again, a new depth inhabits them. They see things differently.

A source surges beneath the future temple that the prophet Ezekiel contemplates. Living waters sing beneath the stones. And this changes everything. The imposing structure is powerless against this stirring of the depths. The prophet looks at it stunned and delighted: "a stream came out from under the temple threshold and flowed eastwards, since the temple faced east. The water flowed from under the right side of the temple, south of the altar..." (Ezek. 47, 1). Where waters flow, life swirls with its unpredictable freshness. Ezekiel finds himself invited by his guide to walk into the stream whose current grows ever stronger and to wade across it. He does so. The water is only ankle deep. A thousand cubits further and it reaches his knees. Another thousand and it is up to his waist. Still another thousand and it becomes impossible to cross. He has to swim. It has become no longer simply a stream, but an uncrossable river (Ezek. 47, 5). And along its course life blossoms: trees, flowers, and fruits cover its shores.

And this river, growing ever stronger and wider, finally empties into the Dead Sea. And at this contact even the Dead Sea itself becomes wholesome! Its wide expanse begins to teem with life: it swarms with all kinds of fish. From En-Gaddi to En-Eglayim fishermen spread their nets (Ezek. 47, 10). The sea has lost its sinister, monotonous quality. It is no longer a motionless sheet of water glistening like a steel blade in the hollow of a rocky landscape. It scintillates now, surrounded as it is by green foliage. And at night, as the sun sinks behind the cliffs, the boats of fishermen linger over its fecund waters into the night.

All night long, Ezekiel listens to the bubbling of life-giving waters. They flow and touch the deepest parts of his self. And what was at first only a murmur now roars like a mountain torrent. The geometrist could not restrain the poet for very long. Life is always stronger. The vision of the temple measured out in such detail has vanished, borne away by the life-giving current. It has been transformed into a new Genesis. A new heart now beats in the breast of the person.

Have we exhausted the meaning of this great prophetic vision? There seems to be no possible comparison between the surging of these liberated and life-giving waters toward the vast, wide sea and the restricted, measured reconstruction of the temple. And yet a profound bond unites these two realities. A bond that nothing and no one can tear asunder. We have placed the water and the temple in opposition; we must now join them together to grasp the full meaning of what is taking place. If the current of living waters flows beyond the temple boundaries and into the sea, recreating all things in its passage, it is nonetheless beneath the temple and there only that it finds its source. Here we are touching what is essential to the vision. We cannot separate the source from the temple, the spirit from the institution. No more than we can separate the soul from the body. The soul radiates beyond the body but always through this very body that it animates. So the spirit

of God flows beyond the temple and reaches out to
the universe, but it does so beginning at the temple
which it rebuilds and renews. The life-power of the
spirit moves by way of the institution at the same
time that it extends itself beyond it. The latter must
remain open to the creative power of the spirit and
its overflowing. The institution is for the spirit and
the spirit is for the world.

Chapter 11

A New People

Henceforth, a deep bond exists between Yahweh and the "broken-hearted." The deportees gradually discover that this is the same reality underlying the covenant itself. The covenant seen as a bond of love, as a feast of the heart. On a clear Oriental night, Abraham saw the sign of his countless descendants shining in the skies. From the depths of their dark night, the exiles see the golden ring of the covenant shine forth anew.

They are so overwhelmed by this discovery that they have the impression of finding themselves in the presence of an entirely new covenant. To be sure, this covenant in no way resembles the one they had been taught. It does not take hold of people by the exterior fringes of their person simply because they belong to an ethnic or political group. Rather it takes hold of them in the most intimate part of their being: It reaches the heart:

> See, the days are coming—it is Yahweh who
> speaks—when I will make a new covenant with the
> House of Israel (and the House of Judah), but not a
> covenant like the one I made with their ancestors on
> the day I took them by the hand to bring them out of
> the land of Egypt ... This is the covenant I will make
> with the House of Israel ... Deep within them I will
> plant my Law, writing it on their hearts. Then I will
> be their God and they shall be my people. There will
> be no further need for neighbor to try to teach neigh-
> bor, or brother to say to brother. "Learn to know
> Yahweh"! No, they will all know me, the least no
> less than the greatest ... (Jer. 31, 31–34).

This message from Jeremiah, picked up by his dis-
ciples, circulated among the deportees. It is a revo-
lutionary message. Until then, the covenant had
been bound to the historical and liberating event of
Exodus: a political and physical reality as well as a
moral and religious event. It was truly the founding
event, the deed which had established Israel as the
people of Yahweh. Since then the entire life of
Israel—its laws, its institutions. its rituals and its
feasts—was referred to it. And the covenant rested
on this tremendous event.

And now the prophecy of Jeremiah, like that of
Ezekiel (Ezek. 36, 25–27; cf. 11, 19), breaks with this
hallowed representation of the history of salvation.
It proclaims a new economy of salvation. The covenant of Yahweh with his people will no longer be con-
nected with past events; it will establish itself directly in the heart of the person. The founding experience will be one disclosed in the most intimate
part of one's being.

From this new perspective, one no longer looks

backward for great beginnings but forward and within oneself. The focus is displaced. From the historical genesis of the covenant, it shifts toward an interior genesis. Henceforth, what counts is to come from the depths of one's being.

> No need to recall the past,
> no need to think about what was done before.
> See, I am doing a new deed... (Is. 43, 18–19).

Who better than the exiled are capable of understanding such a language? For them, this new economy of salvation has already begun. They are living it. In the midst of the collapse of everything that served as a link to what was most sacred in their past, they are given the unsurpassable experience of the nearness of Yahweh. The bond which is set there between God and the "broken-hearted" is something very original. It is not the result of any past deed; it does not depend on anything external. This bond is realized only in the encounter of the great poverty of a devastated heart with the passionate spirit of Yahweh. It holds together by itself. It is sufficient unto itself. It is the new covenant.

This covenant frees persons from everything which tended to make them simple elements of a social grouping or their history. It places them into a direct and personal relationship with God. And through this, it confers on individuals a value which no power can annex; an indefeasible zone of freedom is conquered.

And yet this covenant is not struck between an individual and God alone; it is not simply something which develops in an interiority cut off from the world. If it frees persons from the hold of the group, its totalitarian pretense, and its narrowmindedness, it is in order to open them up to a new community, one without frontiers. No doubt this covenant can only be set in the great solitude of a "broken heart." But, paradoxically, this solitude is the way to authentic communion. Far from closing persons in on themselves, such an experience can indeed only be realized if it fosters an ever greater receptivity.

This receptivity must be exercised first of all toward the prophet. Between Yahweh and the "brokenhearted" stands this man, like them yet different, who speaks in the name of Yahweh. A human relationship must be established. The prophet, in order to be heard, must be understood. The word must take the route of this humble human acknowledgment.

But at the same time, another level of relationship is established. Among all those who live this experience, this same dispossession of self, new bonds are created. The "broken-hearted" seek one another out and meet. The word they have received brings them together. They discover that they share the same quality of heart, the same poverty, the same expectation and hope. An in-depth dialogue opens up: The poor speak in the night. Out of this communion is born the new people of God.

Basing itself on this experience of communion, the new covenant shatters the traditional understanding of the people of God. The latter is no longer defined by its belonging to an ethnic or political group; nor is it determined by blood, race, or institutions. It is not even linked any longer to an initiatory rite. Everything which restricted the people of God to a clan or to any kind of grouping is destroyed. The new people of God finds its origin in a certain quality of heart, in an experience of limitless communion. It consists of the "poor" of Yahweh, of those who have the "broken heart" and who have opened themselves to the spirit.

The notion of the people of God is thus freed from any particularism. This experience, it is true, is still realized only in the night. It is lived as expectation and in unqualified receptivity. But what appears here in a preliminary way is of concern not only for the future of Israel but for that of all of humanity as well. These men and women who learn to live close to their hearts realize, in their night, a breakthrough to the intimate and the universal. What they catch a glimpse of is the ultimate truth of the people of God and the ultimate truth of our humanity as well. The new covenant reveals a new order of relationships not only between men and women and God, but likewise between men and women themselves. It becomes the principle for universal human communion.

Israel is not the only people to have enabled humanity to attain the universal. The great philosophers had discovered the "logos" or reason, as an essential and universal dimension of being. And this coming to awareness also represented a great moment in the history of humankind: a great opporutnity for humanity. In discovering themselves as persons in their possession of the "logos," that is to say in their access to speech and their ability to grasp the essence of things, men and women not only lifted themselves above nature and animality but also above their own particularisms. They acquired a universal human space. However, this coming to consciousness of the Greek philosophers had its limitations. It can never be forgotten that it was in the name of this same power of reason and its superior value that philosophers justified slavery. For, they would say; if all men and women possess the power of reason they do not do so equally; they do not therefore have the same dignity. "The slave," writes one of them, "is someone who shares in reasoning power in a way strong enough to perceive it but not strong enough to truly possess it." It is not surprising that such an ideal of humanity led Greek wisdom to a sort of lifelessness of which Sophism and skepticism were signs. Due to its very rationalism, Hellenistic thought increasingly estranged itself from the deep sources of communion. It ultimately could not resist the mystery religions coming from the East which corresponded precisely to this need for communion.

It is true that Plato had attempted to assume Eros and associate it with the highest forms of the spirit by directing the energies of communion toward the contemplation of supramaterial, suprasensible beauty. But the Platonic Eros is an ascensional power which liberates persons only by removing them from the material and living world and from the world of history. In the final analysis, it is nothing more than an enthusiasm and a lyricism directed toward the world of ideas. This celestial Eros becomes lost in abstract universals, leaving the earthly Eros far behind, abandoning it to its own archaism. The latter is not saved. No matter what it may seem to be at first sight, the Platonic theory of love does not abolish the basic dualism which serves as inspiration for the master's thought. It does not truly assume the world of matter and life with all its obscure drives. Love, for Plato, is universalized only through disincarnation, the dropping of the body. It is not a love of being but of the idea. Such a love is unaware of beings in their personal and collective history. In truth it knows no one and is in communion with no one.

It was to be Israel's privilege to open men and women to the universal by personalizing them. The prophets return persons to the center of their living being at its most sensitive point: They lead them back to their own "hearts" where they are truly themselves: with their hidden, passionate, and painful lives and with all their capacity for communion. And this is where a new covenant is struck in a remarkable encounter of the total person with the passionate spirit of Yahweh.

By celebrating the wedding of the spirit of God with the "heart of flesh," the prophets endow the new people of God with a universal dimension. Now, nothing limits it in space or time. Abraham's descendants can harvest all the stars in the sky. They are to be found wherever one finds the "brokenhearted," open wide to the wonderment of the spirit.

Chapter 12

The Promised Land

> See, I am doing a new deed, even now it comes to
> light; can you not see it? Yes. I am making a road in
> the wilderness, paths in the wilds (Is. 43, 19).

Peoples, like individuals, draw the images and
symbols that they use to decipher and build their
future out of their past history. For exiled Israel the
symbol of the Exodus toward the promised land was
like the key that unlocks a prisoner's cell: the doors
open and light floods in. Not yet liberation, but a
promise of return. A new exodus is heralded, one
more marvelous than the first. And beneath this
great image of their dreams, the exiles sense a new
breath of air issuing out of the natal earth. From the
depths their entire being comes to life again.

The proclamation of the new exodus is accompanied by an overflow of outward signs and pro-
digies. Water streams over the desert; dry ground is
transformed into a running spring; the steppe becomes a garden of Eden, with all kinds of trees grow-

ing in it. The sun no longer scorches the earth, nor does the wind dry it up. Green pastures appear, the wild beasts give glory to God, and the people of Yahweh, liberated, march forward victoriously on straightened highways. They march "toward the wheat, the new wine, and the oil, towards herds of sheep and cattle" (Jer. 31, 12). Begun by Jeremiah, the theme of the new exodus is taken up and orchestrated by the second Isaiah who make it his own and gives it epic imagery. This image of the new exodus with its wondrous and carnal aspects stands in sharp contrast to the spiritual experience of the exile. We seem to be far from a return to the heart and an approach to the living God by way of divestment and poverty!

And yet there is a deep bond between these new images and those of the night crossing. By presenting the new exodus in its most wonder-provoking light, the prophets proclaim an intervention of Yahweh which will eclipse everything he had done so far; no mere repetition of the past, but something completely new.

As a matter of fact, the prophets do not describe the promised land; They dream it. This marvelous land rising out of desert lands and wastes is primarily a land teeming with life. Grain, wine, and oil are in abundance. Herds and flocks, too. And what great springs! Everywhere they sing (Is. 61, 18; 49, 10). Bubbling waters, milky waters, at once refreshing and nourishing. Here the imagery acquires a new depth, an intimacy. This land becomes a place of peace. It is a good place to dwell in. There is no violence, oppression, or conflict of any kind. Right, justice, and peace reign (Is. 60, 18). The houses are secure, the homes quiet. Here human relationships recover their lost tenderness. In short, this land has become a reconciled universe, a new Eden where everyone is fraternal.

The land has also become hierophantic, filled with the knowledge of Yahweh. It no longer needs the light of the sun during the day nor that of the moon at night; it is illumined from within. Yahweh himself is its sun. Dreamt of in this way, the new promised land symbolizes a fullness of being and of life where wounds and brokenness are completely absent and in which men and women rediscover universal communion.

We have no problem recognizing in this prophetic image the great archetype at work in all myths of origins, that of a primal unity within which the sacred, the natural, and the human are still in divine harmony. This archetype is responsible for the image's seductiveness. We should not be surprised, then, to see the prophets using the archaic powers of dreams to work upon the souls of the exiles. These forces operate at the source of human experiences that are at once most carnal and the most spiritual. This new immersion into humanity's archaic self here becomes the way to a prophetic exploration of our destiny. The image of the new promised land does not simply entail a return to mythical man, some fascination with a lost unity. To be sure, it meets persons at the most obscure point of their desire; it speaks to them in the language of their most secret dreams; but it does so in order to open them to their most authentic becoming. The great covenant which will reunite nature, men and women, and God in one and the same communion is no longer to be sought back in some primordial time. It acquires the meaning of a future to be built.

All these wonderful images of a new exodus ultimately find their point of reference in the deep experience of exile. They indeed express a return to the land of the forefathers, but this return is itself symbolic language for an interior journey toward "the new heart" where there is no longer any hatred, where inexhaustible sources of tenderness spring forth and bright mornings shine. Such depth and transparency is available only to those who have passed through the "great abyss":

> Did you not dry up the sea,
> the waters of the great Abyss,
> to make the seabed a road
> for the redeemed to cross?
> Those whom Yahweh has ransomed return,
> they come to Zion shouting for joy ... (Is. 41, 10–11).

This great abyss made dry by Yahweh's breath not only represents the Red Sea whose waters parted to allow for the Hebrews' passage out of Egypt. It is the soul stripped of its self-sufficiency and its idols, humbled to the ground and returned to its original depths. Thus "seabed" becomes a path of freedom and of communion.

To reconcile men and women with their interior archeology while opening them up to the universal is one characteristic of a great symbol. The promised land dreamt of at one's depths is one of these symbols. It gives the exiled people an opportunity to get in touch with its carnal roots again, while at the same time freeing it from its particularisms. The land is in fact no longer a narrow or closed reality; it is now opened to the most remote peoples. They throng toward it. And the new Jerusalem opens up in all directions.

A new relationship between Israel and the world is created here thanks to the prophetic image of the promised land. The people of Yahweh are invited to find their place in the universe and to better understand themselves by discovering the meaning of the land and of the world: "Have you not understood how the earth was founded?" (Is. 40, 21). "Lift your eyes and look. Who made these stars if not he who drills them like an army, calling each one by name?" (Is. 40, 26). These words, addressed as they are to men and women who have lost everything, even the land itself, may surprise and shock us at first. Aren't they out of order and beside the point? Is this really the right time to evoke the power and splendor of creation and invite men and women to gaze at it in wonder? What relationship can exist between the anguished waiting of the deportees and the mute universe or the silence of the galaxies? Why this detour through the stars? And yet these words are also words of salvation.

Indeed, there could be nothing more important and salvific for the people of God than to know and to acknowledge that its insignificant history and its election has its basis in the great creative call and that the one who leads them is also the shepherd of the stars. "I hid you in the shadow of my hand, when I spread out the heavens and laid the earth's foundations and said to Zion, 'You are my people'" (Is.

41, 16). The same creative word established both the universe and the covenant. The latter is not something superadded or a kind of afterthought. It is linked to the foundation of the world. It therefore shares its solidity. To destroy it one would need to destroy the universe, annul creation itself. The fall of Jerusalem and the destruction of the kingdom of Judah marked the end of a little world. But the universe, the great universe, continues. Each morning the sun rises and every night the stars also begin to shine; Yahweh calls them and they all answer as on that first day. This denotes the permanency of creation. In the absence of every other sign, this permanency attests to the fidelity of Yahweh, his design and purpose, his covenant. God is faithful, "he does not grow tired or weary" (Is. 40, 28). He rejects nothing that he has done. What he called forth once, he calls forth forever. All things reverberate with fidelity. Not in the clamor of words but in the secret of their existence. Creation lives on—and with it the covenant.

Linked to the creative act, the covenant at the same time takes on the dimensions of the universe; it is wedded to its immensity and universality. It is not only inseparable from the genesis of the world, but it is also the latter's real finality. Nothing is willed apart from it. Everything that exists finds in it its destination and reason for being. It is the meaning of the world. In it everything holds together. The Milky Way is truly "the luminous sister of the white waterways of Canaan" (Apollinaire. *Alcools*.).

This is what the new heart perceives. It hears

these words from Yahweh: "Your spouse will be your creator" (Is. 54, 5). Words of incredible import, of limitless implication, binding together the covenant and all of creation. It is not by turning in on themselves that men and women rediscover the certainty of their election, but by opening themselves to the call of the creator. Let them cease running around in circles within themselves, clenching themselves against their destiny! They must instead look higher and further than the narrow limitations of their own story. They are called to take on the dimensions of the universe, to listen to the song of the world, and open themselves in wonderment to a destiny which enfolds and extends beyond them on every side! The new promised land is of universal dimensions.

Stripped of everything that was peculiar to it, thrown in the midst of pagan nations, Israel had never been so free to adopt such an awareness or to pursue such an about-face. Today it can hear the song of the world.

Chapter 13

Console My People

More than fifty years have elapsed: How many of the deportees are left? Yet, in the heart of the faithful remnant, expectation remains keen. Sons and daughters have been born in this land of exile. They too share in this expectation. They watch the signs of the times.

For a long time now history seemed to have come to a standstill. Like a sea of still waters. It blends into the exasperating monotony of daily life. Nothing happens. Babylon reigns. And this uncontested reign seems to be marked with the seal of eternity.

But suddenly in the first half of the sixth century before our era, on the other side of the surrounding mountains, toward the East and from the Fertile Crescent, a world is set in motion. A mysterious power stirs on the high plateaus of Iran. A spirit breathes. A new religion makes its appearance. The world, Zarathustra teaches, has become the arena for a struggle between light and darkness. This

struggle, inscribed within the web of creation, reso-
nates in the hearts of men and women. And each one
is invited, from the depths of their night, to begin
moving toward the light.

A new political movement also begins to emerge. It
is incarnated in a man of genius: Cyrus, the young
king of Anshan. At the head of the Persian warriors,
he rises up against the violent and cruel despot As-
tragus of Mede. The struggle against tyranny has
begun. For eight years, the forces of Cyrus assault
the Median empire. Finally, Ecbatana, the capital,
falls into his hands. Cyrus becomes the king of the
Medians and the Persians, now one empire. What
might have seemed until then simply a change of
dynasty suddenly takes on worldwide dimension.
Cyrus seizes Sardinia and brings the Lydian kingdom to an end. The Greek coastal cities are likewise
conquered. Cyrus then turns north and unifies
under his sceptre all the nomadic tribes of this immense region extending from present-day Russian
Turkestan to Afghanistan. Master of the Orient from
Cilicia to the Persian Gulf, he now surrounds the
Chaldean empire.

This new conqueror not only distinguishes himself
by his military genius. He also shows himself to be a
man who is politically liberal and respectful of
peoples and their beliefs. His deeds are animated by
a desire for peace and reconciliation. There are no
exterminations or reprisals. The conquered Croesus
is simply sent away to live under surveillance in a
palace in Ecbatana. The divinities of the conquered
are also respected and their temples spared or re-
built. In this, Cyrus distinguishes himself from all

the despots who had imposed themselves in the Orient until then. He affirms himself as the liberator of the oppressed peoples of Babylon.

The news spread rapidly throughout the Oriental world. It even penetrated the heart of the Chaldean empire and reached the "debris of Israel" scattered throughout the plains of the Euphrates. The exiles hear about the liberator and lean his name. And now they are on the lookout for news. The world has a new face. The wind turns and this time it seems on the right side. As after a long and harsh winter, the dormant earth awakens: The buds blossom, the countryside turns green again, torrents spring to life, and the birds sing in this new light. Spring has arrived. And Israel's heart quivers. What was unthinkable only yesterday now becomes possible. Isn't this Yahweh's breath blowing through history? The exiles ask themselves. They remember Isaiah's prophecy. Two hundred years ago, he announced a great theophany which would put an end to all oppression and inaugurate an era of peace and justice in the world:

> The people that walked in darkness
> has seen a great light:
> on those who live in a land of deep shadow
> a light has shone.
>
> You have made their gladness greater,
> you have made their joy increase;
> they rejoice in your presence
> as men rejoice at harvest time,
> as men are happy when they are dividing the spoils.
>
> For the yoke that was weighing on him,
> the bar across his shoulders,

the rod of his oppressor,
these you break as on the day of Midian.

For all the footgear of battle,
every cloak rolled in blood,
is burned,
and consumed by fire ... (Is. 9, 1-4).

How often have they read this prophecy! They
know it by heart. Very quickly they recognized
themselves in this people groping in the darkness,
these inhabitants of a land of deep shadows. People
of the night, crushed by darkness, ever on the alert
for the first rays of dawn. And suddenly without any
transition, the bright daylight of noon breaks
through! As on the first day of Genesis. Only yesterday, everything was so gloomy. One could see nothing lying ahead. And with one stroke the night disappears. The supernatural light announced by the
prophets now shines for them. And this is incredibly
true. Their hearts beat faster, they are stricken with
emotion by the wild possibility that perhaps their
liberation is near, that they will see it and return to
their country. And more than one turns his or her
face away to weep with joy.

A shadow remains, however. Only one doubt. But
a considerable one for one who bases his hope on
Yahweh's word alone. The marvelous light of which
Isaiah speaks is bound to the birth of a child from
the race of David. It is a son of Israel who is to establish the reign of justice and peace on earth. He is to
inherit the wisdom of Solomon, the bravery of David,
and the religious spirit of Moses and the patriarchs.
In short, all the qualities of his ancestors will shine
in him:

> For there is a child born for us,
> a son given to us
> and dominion is laid on his shoulders;
> and this is the name they give him:
> Wonder Counselor, Mighty God,
> Eternal Father, Prince of Peace.
> Wide is his dominion
> in a peace that has no end,
> for the throne of David
> and for his royal power,
> which he establishes and makes secure
> in justice and integrity ... (Is. 9, 5-6).

The prophecy concerning the coming of a just king is even more explicit: "A shoot springs from the stock of Jesse, a scion thrusts from his roots ..." (Is. 11, 1).

But the man through whom freedom comes at this historical moment is not a son of Israel. Cyrus is a pagan. So is it truly the spirit of Yahweh which is passing by? This light, is it truly that of the day of Yahweh? Is the promised joy finally permissible? The exiles hesitate and discuss it. They are confused.

It is then that a voice arises from their midst. It speaks in the name of Yahweh. It is no longer the voice of the prophet Ezekiel (which has become still), but a new voice. And what does it say?

> "Console my people, console them."
> say your God.
> "Speak to the heart of Jerusalem
> and call to her
> that her time of service is ended,
> that her sin is atoned for ... (Is. 40, 1-2).

A new prophet has arisen. Someone who drew his inspiration from the night. One exile among others. History has not retained his name. He is referred to as Second Isaiah. Now this prophet without a name, without civil status, without a face, sweeps away all remaining doubts. He proclaims that the arm of Yahweh is at work in what is currently taking place in the Orient. If, on the one hand, he does not explicitly state the name of the liberator, on the other hand he nevertheless designates him without equivocation as the one whom Yahweh himself has called: "Who roused from the East him that victory hails at every step? . . . Who is the author of this deed if not he who calls the generations from the beginning? I, Yahweh . . ." (Is. 41, 2, 4). The conqueror of Sardinia, the man about whom the entire Orient is talking and who swoops from victory to victory is truly Yahweh's chosen instrument; he is the liberator that has been announced:

> I roused him from the north to come,
> from the rising sun I summoned him by name.
> He has trampled the satraps like mortar,
> like a potter treading clay . . . (Is. 41, 25).
> My beloved will perform my pleasure
> with Babylon and the offspring of the Chaldeans (Is. 48, 14).

This is certainly something new and completely unexpected. No one had foreseen it: "I, yes I myself, have spoken and summoned him. brought him and prospered his plans" (Is. 48, 15). Yes, may it be made known and loudly proclaimed! Cyrus is the chosen one of the almighty. The prophet no longer hesitates to name him. And to whomever is taken aback by this, he recalls Yahweh's sovereign freedom. No one can make claims on the creator of the universe. He is free to call whom he wishes. He is the God of all; and his will to save extends to all. Israel must not then be taken aback to see him call upon a pagan to realize his purposes. This election is as completely gratuitous as that of Israel:

> Thus says Yahweh,
> the Holy One, he who fashions Israel:
> Is it for you to question me about my children
> and to dictate to me what my hands should do?
> I it was who made the earth,
> and created man who is on it
> I it was who spread out the heavens with my hands
> and now give orders to their whole array.
> I it was who roused him (Cyrus) to victory... (Is. 45, 11–13).

It is not the first time in the history of the people of God that a pagan king has thus been designated as the chosen instrument of Yahweh. Once before Nebuchadnezzar, the king of Babylon, had been presented by Jeremiah and Ezekiel as the executor of the high deeds of Yahweh. But the election of Cyrus belongs to another order of greatness. This is due to the importance of the mission entrusted to him. Not only will he conquer Babylon but he will also rebuild Jerusalem and the temple and will repatriate the deportees (Is. 44, 28; 45, 4). He will be the "shepherd" of Yahweh, the one who gathers his scattered flock and leads it to full security. He will be the artisan of the peaceful reign of Yahweh. And the prophet does not hesitate to call Cyrus the "anointed" one (Is. 45, 1) of Yahweh, that is to say his messiah. This title had initially been reserved for the kings of Israel and of Judah because of the anointment by which they were consecrated. Cyrus is also subject of a consecration by Yahweh.

But the true meaning of this choice and this consecration is as follows: "It is for the sake of my servant Jacob, of Israel my chosen one, that I have called you by your name, conferring a title though you do now know me ..." (Is. 45, 4). Thus the sudden arrival of Cyrus on the world scene, his victories, his reign, all this is willed with Israel uniquely in mind. Ultimately, the true chosen one of God is Israel. History moves forward on its behalf. In the events that are in the process of changing the face of the Orient, the exiles can thus see, after so many years without any signs, the almost tangible proof of the presence of Yahweh to his people and can rediscover the exalting certitude of their election.

A serious question arises at this point. Doesn't this awareness of the presence of Yahweh on the level of the most current and the most external events constitute a step backwards? What relationship can there be between this reign of God which moves forward in the shambles of the victories of Cyrus and that which appeared out of the trial of the exiles in the night, to the "broken-hearted"? Are we still speaking the same language? Patiently the exiles had learned, thanks to the prophets, to listen to Yahweh in silence and in obscurity. And now they have ears only for the stunning testimonies of his action! They who saw no signs now suddenly discover them in profusion. And Yahweh seems to support this and encourage them in this direction: "I have not spoken in secret, in some corner of a darkened land. I have not said to Jacob's descendants, 'Seek me in chaos'" (Is. 45, 19). These words have a strange resonance when one remembers those

a new heart, a desire for power! And what a temptation it is! The liberation is now close at hand. One
must keep a very cool head in order not to act a little
tipsy in moments like this. Cyrus is at the gates. The
most recent news reports that he has crossed the
Tigris near Arbela. Babylon, as if paralysed, does
not react. Nabonidus, the weak Nabonidus, third
successor to Nebuchadnezzar, remains inactive.
Even more, because of his religious policies, he suc-
ceeds in alienating the Babylonian clergy and part
of the population. Everyone's eyes thus turn to the
East. Cyrus does not rush. He knows that time is on
his side. Yet a little while and Babylon, the capital,
will open its gates and welcome him as its liberator.

"The history of the world," writes Hegel, "is that
last judgment of the world." The German philosopher
did not hesitate in hailing the conqueror of Jena
as a figure of the absolute spirit. In a letter
dated Monday, October 13, 1806, he wrote to Niet-
hammer: "The day when Jena was occupied by the
French and the Emperor Napoleon entered its gates,
I say the Emperor—that soul of the world . . . (Hegel,
Correspondance, 1785–1812, 1962, pp. 114–15). Will
the exiles from Judah yield in the enthusiasm of their
liberation to this facile reading of history? The
young Hegel could easily allow himself to be fasci-
nated by the prestigious figure of the Emperor. But
what can anyone know of the spirit of God until they
have had their heart "broken"? One who has struggled in hand-to-hand combat with God all night long
and has been blessed by him limps in the morning
when he takes to the road again; he or she then
knows that the spirit of God also manifests itself in

the poverty of a wounded existence and that it dwells in the "broken-hearted."

It is precisely this experience which ultimately restrains the exiles from triumphalism and which leads the prophet himself to look beyond and further than the recent conqueror (worthy as he might be) and to read history at a deeper level. Whether it likes it or not, Israel bears the marks of its exile; it emerges from its great torment crippled and with eyes that are not easily blinded by the twinkling grandeurs of history.

Before these eyes which scrutinize the future, the figure of this great leader gradually disappears and another, mysterious and overwhelming, makes its appearance: that of the perfect servant of Yahweh. A new order of greatness emerges at this point, one not to be compared to any military of political grandeur. "The saints," writes Pascal, "have their empire, their splendor, their victory, their luster, and need no greatness of the flesh or the mind with which they have no relation, neither adding to them nor taking from them. They are seen by God and the angels, not by bodies nor inquiring minds: God suffices them" (Pascal, *ibid.*, p. 321).

It is toward this mysterious figure of the perfect servant of Yahweh that we must now turn if we want to follow the prophetic and spiritual experience of the exile to its climax.

Chapter 14

An Ultimate Prophecy

His is a paradoxical mission, indeed, this anonymous prophet of the end of the exile. He must, on the one hand, celebrate the exploits of a great leader and, on the other, prepare the spirit of his people to accept a figure bound for humiliation and failure. This twofold task no doubt corresponds to two different moments between which the prophet witnessed a setback. Cyrus indeed freed the deportees, as he announced he would. But the return from exile fell short of the great event so longed for. It did not accomplish the gathering of all of Israel nor the rallying of pagan nations to the one God. Many of the deportees, satisfied with their material condition, preferred to remain in exile. As for the nations, they were not converted. After this double setback, the prophet reflects on his message; he takes it up again from a new perspective, henceforth placing his hopes on a mysterious and future figure to come. Four songs will lead him to an ever more intimate ap-

105

proach to this figure. They have been called the "Songs of the Suffering Servant."

From the very beginning of the first song, the figure of the servant is viewed as clearly distinct from that of the great warrior. The servant does not engage in warfare. His mission is to teach righteousness and truth to the nations.(Is. 42, 1) For this purpose, he has received the spirit of Jahweh (Is. 42, 1). This universal and spiritual mission places him directly in the prophetic line. He acquits himself of his lineage without any outward splendor or violence of any kind. His way is one of gentleness and infinite patience:

> He does not cry out or shout aloud,
> or make his voice heard in the streets.
> He does not break the crushed reed,
> nor quench the wavering flame (Is. 42, 2-3).

By behaving in this way, the servant faithfully fulfills his mission (Is. 42, 3); he works to establish the reign of Yahweh and his justice on the order of greatness proper to it. He does so with courage and without weakness or any detour. Respecting the wavering flame and not breaking the crushed reed, "he will neither waver, nor be crushed" (Is. 42, 4). He advances straightforwardly with great strength of soul, until true justice is established on earth (Is. 42, 4). Moreover, "the islands are awaiting his law" (Is. 42, 4). The "islands," that is to say, the most distant peoples, the extremities of the earth.

Then, in the second part of this first Song, comes the solemn declaration of the servant's investiture: "I, Yahweh, have called you to serve the cause of right; I have taken you by the hand and formed you..." (Is. 42, 6). As with all the great artisans of the purposes of God, the servant is a chosen one, a person set apart. His mission becomes more focused. It is twofold: it concerns both Israel and the pagan nations. The servant will renew Yahweh's covenant with his people and, at the same time, he will shed a light that will enlighten and liberate all of humanity (Is. 42, 6). He, too, will also be a liberator; but he will liberate with light. His mission will be one of light alone. He will open the eyes of the blind, free captives from prison and those who live in darkness from the dungeon (Is. 42, 7).

The horizon widens. The road to the sea opens wide for the servant. Heir to the spirit of the prophets, a great missionary zeal carries him. It is to the peoples beyond the seas that he addresses himself at the beginning of the second song: "Islands, listen to me, pay attention remotest peoples..." (Is. 49, 1). This time the servant speaks; he introduces himself by making known how he has been predestined: "Yahweh called me before I was born, from my mother's womb he pronounced my name..." (Is. 49, 1). This first confidential revelation brings to mind the vocation of Jeremiah. But the images that follow would evoke the destiny of a warrior if the "mouth" of the servant were not mentioned:

> He made my mouth a sharp sword,
> and hid me in the shadow of his hand.
> He made me into a sharpened arrow,
> and concealed me in his quiver (Is. 49, 2).

These warlike images bring us into an atmosphere very different from that of the first song. Here a combative atmosphere reigns. The servant's mission will not be accomplished without struggle. He needs to be armed. And his arms will be the spoken word. He will experience moments of depression before the apparent futility of his efforts. The certitude of his election will just suffice to sustain him against discouragement:

> He (Yahweh) said to me, "You are my servant
>   (Israel)
> in whom I shall be glorified";
> while I was thinking, "I have toiled in vain,
> I have exhausted myself for nothing..." (Is. 49, 3-4).

For the first time the prospect of a difficult task, one without apparent success, makes its appearance in these poems. Yahweh nevertheless remains at the side of his servant and maintains his close friendship: "and all the while my cause was with Yahweh, my reward with my God. I was honored in the eyes of Yahweh, my God was my strength..." (Is. 49, 4). Before the struggles awaiting him, the servant thus strengthens himself in the certitude that God will not abandon him and that his mission has a greatness of its own. It is clear now that this mission extends beyond the simple restoration of Israel. It is part of a wider dimension. Furthermore, it is extended to all men and women and is essentially a religious mission. The salvation which the servant heralds and crafts is devoid of any kind of nationalism. It consists in the gift of light offered to everyone: "It is not enough for you to be my servant, to restore the tribes of Jacob and bring back the survivors of Israel; I will make you the light of the nations so that my salvation may reach to the ends of the earth... (Is. 49, 6).

This light is that of the revelation of Yahweh.
The servant sets himself to listen to this revelation.
The third song introduces us to the intimacy within the life of the servant, to the deep relationship
which he enjoys with Yahweh. Like a docile disciple,
he lets himself be instructed by God. He does not
invent or create his message; he receives it:

> The Lord Yahweh has given me
> a disciple's tongue.
> So that I may know how to reply to the wearied
> he provides me with speech.
> Each morning he wakes me to hear,
> to listen like a disciple.
> The Lord Jahweh has opened my ears (Is. 50, 4).

This message, however, is not a well-learned lesson. It is through life experience that Yahweh
awakens his servant: precisely through the difficul-
ties and the rebuffs that the latter encounters in the
fulfillment of his mission. Having been tested himself, the servant finds just the right words to reach
exhausted hearts.

More and more, the role of this perfect disciple
proves arduous and painful. His docility consists in
assuming it fully without retort or evasion: "For my
part, I made no resistance, neither did I turn away. I
offered my back to those who tore at my beard; I did
not cover my face against insult and spittle..." (Is.
50, 5–6). It is no longer simply a matter of contesta-
tion. The servant is beaten and jeered at. In his misery, he draws strength from the assurance that the
Lord Yahweh is with him and will ultimately intervene in his favor. Strengthened by this hope, he is
able to make his face hard like flint. And he waits.

"My vindicator is here at hand . . . The Lord Yahweh is coming to my help, who dares condemn me?" (Is. 50, 8–9). The third song ends with this cry of trust.

Insulted and ill-treated, the servant hopes for a supernatural intervention that will deliver him from his persecutors. What is dramatic is that Yahweh does not intervene. This is where the scandal and the mystery begin. The meekest man the world has ever known is left prey to the dogs. The fourth and last song leads us into the heart of this scandal and this mystery. The prophet is aware that he will announce something totally unheard of: a mystery combining both opprobrium and glory (Is. 52, 13–15).

The voice of the servant has become silent. This humble and contrite voice which could carry to far-off islands has been brutally reduced to silence. It is now out of the question for the servant to teach. Yet, even so, his mission is not ended. A mysterious role awaits him. He no longer has anything to say or to do. He can only wait at the lowest echelons of human distress and downfall. And what remains for him there is to identify himself with lost humanity. Disfigured beyond human resemblance, "a thing despised and rejected by men," (Is. 53, 3) he has become the man of sorrows: sorrow made man.

People can make an idol of anything: beauty, love, fecundity, power, etc. Of anything but sorrow and humiliation. Idols are always the language of men and women's desires. And men and women do not desire this kind of thing. For these are signs of malediction for them: signs of the absence of the divine, even of its very negation. Biblical people have always felt them as such. The man of sorrows can only be a man "punished, struck by God" (Is. 53, 4): a person from whom God has withdrawn. And, consequently, a sinner, an impious, sinful person. Thus was Job for his friends. And thus the servant of Yahweh for his people.

God is light, power, life, splendor. He manifests his presence on behalf of his friends by surrounding them with his light, his power, his life, and his splendor. Yahweh is neither in darkness, nor in powerlessness, nor in sickness. Nor in failure or death. All of this is where Yahweh is not. Yet this is where the servant finds himself. He has identified himself with the very negation of God. "I am Not-God for you" (Hos. 1, 9): these words of Yahweh to the prophet Hosea can be put in the mouth of the servant; they find their fulfillment here in all their brutality.

This figure is hardly bearable. He is upsetting and scandalous. Respectable folk turn their face away before him. Only those maimed from the great abyss, those who have explored the night of exile, can look at him without losing heart. Something in him draws them and speaks to them. They recognize themselves in him. A mysterious kinship unites them. Doesn't this man of sorrows come from the same arid land? Doesn't he too find root in it, in the shattering experience of devastation and of "broken-heart"? "Like a sapling he grew up in front of us, like a root in arid ground" (Is. 53, 2). This figure "without beauty, without majesty" that Yahweh chose to break appears fraternal to them.

Fraternal and sacred at the same time. It is one

and the same reality with the mystery of the hidden God who dwells in the "broken-hearted." Here the longest night, that of the exiled people and persecuted prophets, becomes transfigured into one mysterious theophany. Yahweh is there precisely where everything cries out his absence. *Especially* there. His presence and his absence are brought together in the silence of this man destined to be scorned and horrendously ill-treated. The signs of our malediction undergo radical change here. Humiliation, suffering, and death cease to be the signs of the absence of God: They become, instead, the signs of his mysterious presence.

The God who reveals himself here does not allow himself to be represented in the forms of Greek beauty. Or in the noble traits of the wise man. Or even less in the luster of almighty splendor. It is the holy and passionate God who appears here. The servant is clean of any sin. There is no falsehood coming from his mouth and no trace of injustice on his hands. He is innocence itself. If he enters into our solitude and our night, if he takes our sin upon himself and offers himself to death, it is because he has allowed himself to be seized by the passion of the holy God for the sinner: he has made his own God's concern to reach the lost. He thus realizes the mysterious coming of the holy God at the heart of our distress and our night. In this, he is more than ever the servant of Yahweh: the one who fulfills his destiny by making it come to birth in the world.

In reading this song that celebrates the passion of the servant, we can ask ourselves the question posed by the important functionary of the Queen of Ethiopia who came to Jerusalem on a pilgrimage: "Tell me, is the prophet referring to himself or someone else?" (Acts 8, 34). No doubt we can appropriately respond: "at once to himself and to another." Everything that the prophet has seen, lived, and suffered during these trying years in the midst of a people chosen yet abandoned comes to the surface in these songs of the servant. "The servant," writes André Neher, "is a child of Israel, born out of the pain of Israel." He is truly the son of the exile, of this passage through the night during which all visible bonds fell apart and men and women found themselves alone, confronted with their own heart. "We had all gone astray like sheep, each taking his own way" (Is. 53, 6). The servant represents the highest expression of the experience of the "broken heart" open to the mysterious purposes of God. He is the exact translation of the awareness that the small remnant has of its mission in the world, at the end of its long process of purification.

The servant, however, cannot be considered as the simple projection, deep as it may be, of the experience of some prophet or of Israel itself. For even if the figure is rooted in this experience, it transcends it. The servant is alone before everyone. Alone because of his shadowless holiness. Alone because of his mission to bear the sins of all. Alone due to the universal scorn that befalls him. Alone, finally, because of the secret and free decision to offer himself for all. At the heart of the servant, there is this act of freedom where he finds himself alone:"he surrendered himself" (Is. 53, 6). The servant belongs to no one. In vain can we try to identify him with a race or a class. He has been cursed and rejected by everyone. Everyone without exception. He is alone against everyone else.

And it is at the very moment that he is rejected by everyone and is absolutely alone that mysteriously he is with everyone, in solidarity with everyone. But this solidarity is no longer that of a class or of a race. In pursuing solitude and night to their utmost limits, the servant has torn himself away from every particular bond, from every particular condition, to come to know only the person's essential poverty before the mystery of God. He becomes the person completely taken up by the mystery of God and completely open to it. He no longer belongs to himself. He belongs to the mystery of God. And this is why he becomes this mystery revealing itself at the heart of our distress and our night.

Cyrus and the servant of Yahweh: two figures that are part of the liberation of the people of God. Both inspired by the spirit, together they create the prophetic vision of history. Cyrus, with his victories but even more with his political and human acumen, works for the temporal liberation of humanity. The servant, through his teaching and his passion, realizes an even deeper liberation. The personality of Cyrus reveals and illustrates the breath of the spirit active in what makes history. That of the servant brings to the surface, in a way that lies beyond this activity and extends to the depths of suffering and failure, a supreme affirmation of the spirit and a final fulfillment of humanity; it demonstrates that the life of the spirit is not one that is frightened by devastation and the night, but that which endures and transfigures them with great patience. It proclaims that history is not humanity's final horizon nor God's final judgment.

Chapter 15

Under the Reign of Caesar Augustus

That day had begun like all others. Jerusalem had been awakened by the sun and the noise of merchants. In shining armor, the Roman cohort was returning from a round. Order reigned. Everyone was about his or her work. And Rome ruled the world.

One man, however, had the feeling that something very important for his people and the future of the world was about to take place. This pious and just man was hastening toward the temple. His name was Simeon. He was a man well on in years, who had meditated quite a bit, and, above all, a man of much hope. At an age when most don't expect anything more than life, he expected everything. His heart overflowed with hope as if he were heir to all the hope accumulated by his people from generation to generation ever since Abraham. Simeon awaited the Consolation of Israel. He was not waiting for it as for something far-off and abstract, but as an event very near, one that he would see himself.

"The Consolation of Israel": This expression had nothing saccharine about it in the mouth of the old man; nor did it evoke some spectacular event, one of those striking deeds that occasionally make peoples tremble. Rather it announced a deep and decisive coming event. Simeon was familiar with the *Book of the Consolation of Israel* by Isaiah. It was about the message contained in this book that he was thinking whenever he spoke of the Consolation of Israel. He had nourished himself with this book day after day, meditating upon *The Poems of the Servant* at great length. He had let himself become penetrated by the spirit that had inspired the prophet. And the spirit itself had taken hold of him. He had revealed to him the greatness and holiness of the coming reign of God. "The Holy Spirit rested on him" (Lk. 2, 25), writes the evangelist Luke, echoing the words of Isaiah (Is. 61, 1–2).

Simeon, therefore, was waiting for the saving Messiah, but not as if for a conquering national hero who would break the yoke of Roman occupation and give Israel its independence and its place among the nations. Nor did he wait for him as for an avenging fire which would purify everything in its path by the strength of its power and its holiness. He waited in the spirit of the poems of the servant. This Messiah would be a man of the spirit. His coming would take place without outward splendor. He would act not with the sword nor with fire, but with words. He would speak words that save and liberate. His message would be addressed to all, even to far-off peoples and pagans. He would bring universal salvation. But he would be challenged. He would experience a tragic destiny: rejected, beaten, reduced to silence, he would be condemned to solitude and humiliation and would be crushed by suffering and beaten to death. And yet his death, even more than his teaching, would open a way of light and peace for all. "On him lies a punishment that brings us peace, and through his wounds we are healed . . ." (Is. 53, 5). This was the consolation of Israel for Simeon.

Ruminating on these serious thoughts and being driven by the spirit, the old man on that day was hastening to the temple. The event could suffer no more delay. He was certain of it. The spirit had assured him that he would see it before his death.

What had he done to deserve such assurance? He had hoped. And he continued to hope, in spite of his weight of years, in spite of the failures and the misfortunes and the mishaps of life. He hoped with the heart of a poor man, one becoming always poorer. His hope was like a flame that the winds of distress bend and flatten and which yet repeatedly returns upright.

Simeon arrived at the temple. And, at the same time, a young couple entered. The woman carried a baby in her arms. It was Mary, accompanied by Joseph, coming to present her child to the Lord and to offer two turtledoves as a sacrifice in conformity with the prescriptions of the law. No one had noticed her. These were ordinary folk without any retinue. Very indistinguishable, ordinary people. The old man Simeon looked at them. He did not know them either. But suddenly a certitude overcame him. He approached the mother, fixed his gaze on the child, and softly, with infinite precaution, he took it in his arms. Then he began to pray out loud, his face glowing:

> Now, Master, you can let your servant go in peace,
> just as you promised;
> because my eyes have seen the salvation
> which you have prepared for all the nations to see,
> a light to enlighten the pagans
> and the glory of your people Israel (Lk. 2, 29–32).

And while Simeon prayed, everything he had read and meditated upon from the *Book of the Consolation of Israel* came back to him with great clarity:

> Here is my servant whom I uphold . . .
> I have endowed him with my spirit
> that he may bring true justice to the nations.
> He does not cry out or shout aloud,
> or make his voice heard in the streets.
> He does not break the crushed reed,
> nor quench the wavering flame (Is. 42, 1–3).
>
> I Yahweh . . . have appointed you
> as a covenant of the people and light of the
>   nations.... (Is. 42, 6)
>
> I will make you the light of the nations
> so that my salvation may reach to the ends of the
>   earth (Is. 49, 6).

The old man had become silent, and with the child in his arms he remained absorbed in deep contemplation. The father and the mother, Saint Luke reports, were filled with wonder over what they had just heard. Mary knew that her child would rule over the family of Jacob. The angel of the Annunciation had told her so. But at this moment she rejoiced to learn that the mission of her son would extend itself even further and that he would be the light of nations.

Simeon, however, continued to remain silent. And, looking at the child, he again saw the image of the suffering servant just as it is described in the *Book of Consolation:*

> The crowds were appalled on seeing him
> —so disfigured did he look
> that he seemed no longer human— (Is. 42, 14).

> a thing despised and rejected my men,
> a man of sorrows and familiar with suffering,
> a man to make people screen their faces;
> he was despised and we took no account of him (Is. 53, 3).

> Harshly dealt with, he bore it humbly,
> he never opened his mouth,
> like a lamb that is led to the slaughterhouse ... (Is. 53, 7).

The old man Simeon knew it: This song of sorrows was also a song of hope, a song of salvation and of victory.

> See, my servant will prosper,
> he shall be lifted up, exalted, rise to great
> heights ... (Is. 52, 13).

> He shall see the lightand be content (Is. 53, 11).

But this victory had to pass through night and death. Turning himself toward the mother, then, Simeon murmured in her ear: "You see this child: he is destined for the fall and for the rising of many in Israel, destined to be a sign that is rejected—and a

sword will pierce your own soul too—so that the secret thoughts of many may be laid bare" (Lk. 2,
34–35).

Mary felt her heart tighten. She had come full of
happiness to present her son to the Lord and offer to
him on this occasion the sacrifice of two turtledoves.
But the words of the old man and the spirit that
inspired him had suddenly lit a tragic light in the
depths of her soul. No, her two turtledoves would not
suffice. These were but pale images. The reality was
something else. Mary looked at the child in the arms
of the old man. The flesh of her flesh would one day
be the victim. Her son would be the disfigured servant that others would be intent on striking down
and who would offer himself up to death for the salvation of all. Oh, why suddenly this violence and
this wrenching in her between the flesh and the
spirit?

The silence was great. Mary heard only the wild
beating of her own heart. She had entered the night
of God. She had never felt so poor, so far away from
God. And never had she been so near.

> You who wanted no sacrifice or oblation,
> prepared a body for me.
> You took no pleasure in holocausts or sacrifices for
>   sin;
> then I said,
> just as I was commanded in the scroll of the book,
> "God, here I am! I am coming to obey your will"
>   (Heb. 10, 5–7; cf. Ps. 40, 7–9).

Epilogue

There has never been an absence of night for believers. Until now, however, it seemed to have been the reserve of an elite, the saints and the mystics. The great masses let themselves be carried by the institution. The church, strong by reason of her hierarchical armature and dominant sociological position, stood high over people with sovereign authority. She possessed the teaching authority, her light shone like a beacon, her sword cut decisively to settle discussions. One needed only to listen and look at her to know what to think and what to do. Everything was clear and sure. But now the institution itself is in the dark. Ousted from its privileged position in the world, the church finds itself challenged from within and from without. And often she finds herself groping to find her way and to emerge with the countenance of the servant. Many, seeing her in this state, are disturbed and confused. They no longer find in her a protective shelter.

Today there are no protected environments. From youth on, men and women are thrown into a world where all kinds of opinions, beliefs, and value systems openly coexist. In this pluralistic world faith can no longer simply be a lesson one has learnt by heart. It requires a constant choice of values and a deepening of existence. It is bound to one's human journey. And no one can make this experience in our place.

Today, as in the time of the exile, the believer is left only with the strengths of his or her heart; he or she is thrown back on his or her essential poverty. God's ways can no longer be known beforehand.

Reduced to essentials, faith becomes an adventure that joins up with the great human adventure. It is no longer something supperadded. The believer journeys with others in the same night. He too must listen to the voices of the world and let himself be challenged by them. And it is at this level of the human journey that he or she is invited to hear the word anew and discover signposts along the way.

This faith reduced to essentials is open to the four winds of the spirit. Today, as in the time of the exile, the spirit breathes. And it breathes in the tumult, precisely in the place where all the walls have crumbled. And this breath is a breath of universality. It renews and assembles men and women coming from the most distant horizons. A new people of God is being born, one which extends beyond traditional boundaries.

"Jeremiah, what do you see?" Yahweh asked his prophet on the eve of the disaster that was to swoop down over Judah. The prophet answered: "I see a branch of the almond tree." And Yahweh said to him: "Well seen! I too watch over my word to see it fulfilled" (Jer. 1, 11–12). The same Hebrew word *sheqed* designates both the watcher and the almond tree. For the prophet the gracious image of the almond tree had nothing reassuring about it. It meant that Yahweh stood watch to execute his threats; it foretold the calamity at hand. But a few years later when the nation was in a state of complete desolation, Yahweh said to Jeremiah: "And as I once watched them to tear up, to knock down, to overthrow, destroy and bring disaster, so now I shall watch over them to build and to plant" (Jer. 31, 28). Did the prophet then remember the branch from the almond tree?

The almond tree is too impatient to wait for the end of winter to announce the coming of spring. It is anxious to blossom. On its bare branches, still clothed with winter chill, bursts new life. Small white flowers appear and shine from the highest branches. In the desolate countryside, the almond tree in flower stands out liminously. And its blossoming branches shine like daybreak in the middle of the night.

Beyond torment and devastation, the word over which God unceasingly keeps vigil always remains the promise. Winter continues to cover our furrows. But already, somewhere, with the church looking on, an almond tree has blossomed.